Defiant Daughters Dancing

Three Independent Women Dance

DEFIANT DAUGHTERS DANCING
Three Independent Women Dance

Rina Angela P. Corpus

The University of the Philippines Press
Diliman, Quezon City

THE UNIVERSITY OF THE PHILIPPINES PRESS
E. de los Santos St., UP Campus, Diliman, Quezon City 1101
Tel. No.: 925-3243 / Telefax No.: 9282558
e-mail: press@up.edu.ph

The National Library of the Philippines CIP Data

Recommended entry:

Corpus, Rina Angela P.
Defiant daughters dancing: three
independent women dance / Rina
Angela P. Corpus.—Quezon City:
The University of the Philippines Press, c2007
180 p.; 23 cm.

1. Feminism and dance—Philippines—History.
2. Dance—Philippines—Social aspects.
3. Ballet—Philippines. I. Title.

GV1703.P5 792.8'09599 2007 P073000451
ISBN 978-971-542-547-6

Book Design by Zenaida N. Ebalan

Printed in the Philippines by Econofast Press

To the *Dadis,* elder sisters and wisest women of my life, for whom dancing in happiness is a way of life.

Contents

Foreword

Moving

Rina Angela Corpus performs a tricky step in this project of telling the story of Philippine contemporary dance, notating its movement against the grain of programmatic choreography. First, she challenges the manner in which histories of dance are crafted from a perspective that precludes the personage of woman as a productive agent in the invention of the art. Second, she takes exception to this historiography by exercising her own form of inclusion and enlistment, foregrounding the practice of three women dance makers who have striven to remake the institution of dance itself and the subjectivities of its faithful. In enacting this complicated turn of the body against the gravity of its tradition, Corpus contrives the argument of independence and its logic of defiance.

This agenda takes her to the usual suspects as well as to surprises within well-laid schemes. We are initiated into the materiality of dance: the masculinist framework of its conception, the dominant repertoire of representations, the Eurocentrism of its artifice, and the violence of disciplined beauty that is to be the horror of the aesthetic. But we are also invited to an alternative performance that is inspired by the impulse to overstep the boundaries of tutelage and engagement. Through the dance practice of Myra Beltran, Kristin Jackson, and Agnes Locsin, the history of dance is not only assured of a vital contemporary expression; it gains a new lease altogether because it is guaranteed a resurgence in terms of the space of its unfolding; the scope of its concerns; and the possibility of its return to native entitlements. In other words, Corpus does not merely repeat the sociological critique of power and rehearse the stance of the political struggle against its regime. As a critic, dance historian, and dancer herself—agencies that are laid bare in conveying this narrative with a view to demystifying its intervention as irrevocably motivated—Corpus conjures the imagination of "independence" as women dance makers ordain lives beyond the balletic habitus and the company structure, hothouses of perfection and professional careers. As she undertakes this task, she makes sense of dance not through technicist or purely hermeneutic means; she attempts to flesh out the gesture of the body through the trope of independence. The latter is construed not as a conquest of frailty or a mastery of human prowess, but an intimation of a fragile but necessary freedom reared in the contingency of a constitution that goes out on a limb.

In the case of Myra Beltran, the body is regrounded, resettled in a dynamic that disrupts the pleasure elicited in a dancing woman and replacing it with the grimace of belabored self-realization. Kristin Jackson for her part shares the self with others in a scheme in which the mentor-apprentice hierarchy is reorganized and in which the Filipino self is situated elsewhere. And Agnes Locsin comes back home to her birthright, south of the capital, where she entangles modern dance of neoethnic inflection with the virtues of cultural work and research. Corpus discerns in all these degrees of exile, a re-location of the privilege of dance and at the same time a co-location of independence among articulations of denial and even of sacrifice, a conjuncture of independent desires, indeed. This argued, she then offers sharp commentary on a possible drift toward the sentimentalization of victimage and solitariness in the quest for the enfranchising fringe, the liberative margin.

This book of Corpus' is a significant sortie into the untrammeled territory of dance, which we realize as we negotiate its itinerary is a neglected field of study in Philippine scholarship. It contributes a methodology that projects itself to be feminist and refigures a technology of the body and the self within the ensemble of the very social energy of moving—against the current of a calling's enervating, but hopefully not exhausted, aspirations.

Patrick D. Flores, Ph.D.
Department of Art Studies
College of Arts and Letters
University of the Philippines
Diliman, Quezon City

Preface

Like an old and seasoned story that insists on its own re-telling, defiance for this writer found expression in the resolve to write about dance, precisely because of and despite its marginality as a field of scholarly study in her chosen discipline of art history. It has been, after all, ten full years since her first foray into dance scholarship, and she still finds herself at it.

Just about four years ago, in between finishing my coursework in art history while professionally involved in advocacy work, I still found some snippets of time to watch, read, and write about dance and the works of women dance artists. My attentive glimpses of the subject soon became the material for more serious inquiries that gave substance to my graduate papers, which would later find print in various academic and cultural journals, and had also largely influenced this book. Coming to the end of my graduate studies in 2003, I also significantly found myself still drawn to dance training, which brought about the decision to re-enter my old ballet school after a four-year respite. My feeling was that I never really left the dance world in the first place. Putting the ballet shoes aside and donning the more intellectual "hat" as an academic, I now find myself seizing whatever space there is to re-align my art-historical framework towards looking at dance, and specifically to look into the stories of independent women dancers—what makes them dance and why they continue to dance—no matter the marginality accorded to their status in the larger art world.

This book springs from various points of departure, all grounded in my personal experiences as a young dancer trained in classical ballet, as a contemporary woman educated in the discipline of art history, and as a feminist writer honed in the state university's tradition of critical thinking and theorizing. This is the narrative of three adult women dancers seen through my lenses as a fourth person, younger in generation than the three subjects but nevertheless trained in the same ballet tradition that the seasoned dance artists under study also passed through. It is this affinity with that traditional dance form that serves as the thread gathering close the generational gaps, geographical distances, and artistic genealogies of the three main players and myself as a fourth performer in this written and collaborative, because shared, performance.

My writing of narratives of three independent women dancers is, needless to say, a continuation of the scholarly inclination towards writing critically about women and dance which I began as an art studies major. It is a topic I continue to take up now as faculty of the UP Art Studies Department, which has traditionally paid more attention to the specialization of visual arts than to dance arts. My initial interest in dance scholarship resulted in my undergraduate thesis, "Reading Mariang Sinderela: Towards a Feminist Discourse of Dance" (1996), a feminist art critical reading of dance choreographed by two young women dancers of the UP College of Music dance program. The stirrings created in sharing that piece to a circle of feminist readers at the University Center for Women's Studies (UCWS) led to the publication of its excerpts in their *Review of Women's Studies.* My subsequent MA thesis,* which formed the initial text of this book project, tackled the narratives of women dancers' histories, coupled with feminist dance criticism. I hope that this continued commitment to write and witness the growth of dance research and scholarship may significantly add depth and breadth to the as yet meager attention given to dance in the country. I was made aware through this research process that while books and reviews have been written on various aspects of Philippine dance, this book would be a first of its kind in the country to openly venture into dance history within the operative lenses of feminist thought and women's studies.

And so gratitude is due to the many souls who enriched the path of this research and writing:

Dr. Patrick Flores and Prof. Basilio Esteban Villaruz for seeing the relevance of writing about women and dance in the academe; my colleagues in the Department of Art Studies who shared their insights into this project, especially Professors Shine Canta, Brenda Fajardo, May Datuin; to Shirley Halili-Cruz, artistic director of the Quezon City Ballet, for the inspiring energy to hone young dancers and whose motherly guidance brought many of us, literally and metaphorically, "up on our toes"; to dance teachers past and present, Teachers Gwen, Jeng, Cookee, Grace, Anna,

* This MA thesis in Art History was originally titled "Defiant Daughters Dancing: Feminist Dance Histories of Three Independent Women Dance-Makers" which received the Outstanding MA Thesis Award from the UP Center for Women's Studies Foundation in March 2006.

Perry Sevidal, and the Swiss Chamber Ballet, for the sheer discipline and love to just share dance; to Mama Duya, Tatay, Tita Didi, Tita Baby, Tita Zor, Tito Rudy, and Tita Te who thoughtfully sent from overseas the rare dance books and materials I needed for this research; to Mama, Papa, Ate Jejel, and JP for the space, trust, and understanding that always allow me to do research and writing sans interruption; to Nanay for the sweet and quiet presence, a balm to harried souls; to Dr. Malou Camagay and Dr. Rhodora Ancheta of UP Press for their encouragement to develop this material; to the spiritual kith and kin I found in the Brahma Kumaris, a spiritual school that taught me the invaluable skill and love for "dancing in one's inner space."

And of course, to the three dance artists—Agnes, Kristin, and Myra—for generously sharing their time and resources in order to impart to this young and probing dance researcher their meaningful life stories, lessons and insights, and their infectious passion for dance.

Finally, to my Baba, whose big heart is the stage where I freely dance.

This research is made richer because of all of you.

Introduction

She effectively undid the past, not just in relation to her own history but also in relation to the traditions of dance that preceded her. The challenge is to continue to ask questions of the past, to be aware of the peristalsis of movement memory that may be intergenerational, and to recognize the potential of the theatre as a museum of the body.

—Carol Brown
in *Migration and Memory: The Dances of Gertrud Bodenwieser*

A Personal Movement: Dissident Gestures into Dance

In this act of writing, I find myself fluidly transgressing boundaries and spaces, sliding between word and gesture, stepping from thought to movement and back again.

As a writer dancing or a dancer writing, I inhabit two worlds that have been separated from each other in the history of Western thought:

mind vs. body, reason vs. emotion, thinking vs. feeling, culture vs. nature, masculine vs. feminine. According to this dualistic thought, the rational mind is to control the non-rational body, reason over emotion, masculine over feminine, and so forth. The privileging of the *One* over the *other* is the consequence of this pervasive binarist notion, and the result has been an imbalance, as it persists to elevate the first and subordinate the other end of the equation.

This project of writing about women in dance is a contribution to the demolition of this very imbalance upheld by patriarchal logic. Inheriting my ballet mistresses' delicate art of balancing between poses and postures, I similarly take up this writing as a crucial performative act, a critical moment of gesturing from this one subjective body: a young contemporary woman largely trained in and exposed to classical ballet, and an art history scholar steeped in the tools of feminist discourse as I refocus the paternal discipline of Western art history towards the project of recovering the marginal field of dance in the canonical history of art, especially the histories of women in the art and dance world. This writing as a performance comes from a sense of self that has been honed and empowered by the experience of both dancing and scholarly studies in dance, realizing that dance has been waylaid in Western academic thinking precisely because it is associated with the body—it is *the other* subordinated half of the aforesaid binarist logic. Seeing too, how women have been historically associated with this *othered* half—woman as body, woman as emotion, woman as nature, woman as non-rational, woman as feminine—and the list of an iniquitous patriarchal typecasting goes on.

It is only comparatively recent—over the past two decades to be precise—that dance has been developed as a field of academic study. Dance has been largely ignored and undervalued as a legitimate subject in the academe, historically not considered a field worthy of critical intellectual scholarship especially in the light of Western dualisms within traditional intellectual epistemologies that uphold the cognitive mind over the corporeal body (Desmond 1997:154; Carter 1998:1).

Women's active engagement in dance—both as dancers and dance makers—has further weighed down the field with a concomitant gender backlash. As dance sociologist Helen Thomas avers, dance has been threefold marginalized from academic and social studies

> first as an art, second as a practice which places the body at the center of its discourse, and third as an activity which is viewed as a predominantly feminine mode of expression and representation. (Thomas 1995, 9)

Nevertheless, this research about dance and the histories of Philippine contemporary women dancers continued through my graduate art history course. It has been an act that proved to be an unveiling of layers upon layers of master narratives that have *othered* dance throughout its written history. With the bulwark of a Western visual arts-centered approach in my graduate art history program, I found this to be a rousing and no less rigorous challenge of recovering spaces for the study of women and dance within academic context. But this is not so much to create another canon, for the Canon of Western Art is already problematic with its privileging of the largely white, heterosexual, Christian man of property—the dominant identity construed to be the natural artist of genius. However, it is in re-inscribing here the particular presence of women dance artists in Philippine contemporary dance that I intend to draw out more questions that would challenge the very notions and constructions that debilitated women in the art world in the first place.

An invocation of feminist politics and scholarship is necessary in this performative act. *Feminisms* is the emergent term used in more progressive academic quarters to imply the multiplicity of women's movements, in the social, political and cultural milieu of contemporary times. More specifically, the discipline of *feminist art history* is here re-functioned as one of the potent tributaries of the *new art histories* in the late 20th century, where the shift of traditional Western art history from object to social context and ideology has brought to the fore questions of structures and systems of social power within which the art world operates and is located (Ferne 1995, 19). The incursion of feminism, psychoanalysis, and theory in the art-historical discipline has thus intensified the mode of historicizing art and its practices, from one that merely authenticates with formalist and iconographic tools, to that which is critical, contextual and discursive in approaching the narratives of the art world. As Patrick Flores posits a more progressive domain of writing a "new history," it is one which

> is able to bear on art history a kind of historiographic perspective that locates the activities of culture as well as those mediations which could be grasped aesthetically in the persistent routine of everyday life. *This covers the oftentimes intimate process of making art—of feeling and performing emotion—and looking at it in determinate settings and processes usually repressed by grand narratives of diachronic periodisation and the parade of masters and masterpieces.* (Flores 1997, 35; italics mine)

Art History, then, becomes the very problematique, the primary object of ideological critique as I foreground in this project the possibility of narrating the stories of art in another way—that which draws upon the emergent and multi-vocal feminist dance histories of three contemporary women dance artists. This makes for a vast departure from Art History's monolithic tradition of privileging the past over the present, which only takes into legitimate account the history of white male geniuses of bygone times. Feminist art historian Griselda Pollock aptly captures the counter-methodology that I summon in this study:

> The political point of feminist art history must be to change the present by means of how we re-represent the past. *That means we must refuse the art historian's permitted ignorance of living artists and contribute to the present-day struggles of living producers.* (Pollock 1988, 310; italics mine)

Instead of upholding an Art History of dead Masters, I choose to re-tell here the current stories of three living figures in Philippine contemporary dance. I also purposively include my voice as a fourth woman, an equally engaged and active performer in this study—not a detached, invisible voice of authority that is traditionally valued in orthodox and androcentric art-historical methodologies and dominant Western epistemologies (Brown 1994, 202). Speaking and unveiling my own voice as a young contemporary woman with specific subjections—a researcher who is also "a real historical individual with concrete, specific desires and interests" (Harding in Brown 1994, 202)—I consciously avoid taking the patriarch's objectivist voice that shrouds itself in the mystery of judgment and authority.

The feminist interventionist strategies in the story of art as proposed by the most influential intellectual mothers of my graduate years, mainly Linda Nochlin (*Why have there been no great women artists*? 1971), Griselda Pollock (*Feminist Interventions in the Histories of Art*, 1988; *Generations and Geographies*, 1996), Astri Wright (*Self Taught Against the Grain*, 1999) and locally, May Datuin (*Home Body Memory*, 2002), are all, however, centered on the visual arts and the subjections and resistances of women therein. I found their methods and perspectives enormously valuable in the way they refined my/our conception of history, not anymore as a grand and seamless narrative of "universal truths" about art, but one of contentious sites of political subjectivities that situate the multiple struggles of women and *othered* identities within the general milieu of a colonialist and masculinist art historical project. But despite this significant grounding in this oppositional paradigm in art history, I still found it most necessary to run several miles further to uncover from my own experiential knowledge and recover in my and others' research and writings that which would resonate the same standpoint about women in the field of dance.

This necessarily leads me back to earlier, untutored endeavors as a budding feminist and college freshman, wide-eyed as I unearthed Christy Adair's book *Women and Dance: Sylphs and Sirens* (1992) in the library of a then small and obscure UP College of Social Work and Community Development. This text proved to be a meaningful find as it traced for me the very genealogical roots of ballet history that helped demystify many ingrained notions about my own ballet training. It also surfaced my feminist inclinations in the study of dance in its critical historicizing of women's roles and resistances in the dominant Western dance world.

In much recent times, however, as I groped for up-to-date materials on feminist dance scholarship, I particularly found a most inspiring affirmation that one cannot, after all, be alone in this disciplinal dissidence in the dance and art world. A relatively recent encounter with the seminal essay of independent dancer-researcher Carol Brown, "Re-tracing our steps: The possibilities for feminist dance histories" in the anthology *Dance History: An Introduction* (1994), affirmed and resonated with the subtitle of this thesis what was already "dancing" in my head at the earlier stage of the research work. The term "feminist dance histories" encapsulated for me the very idea of heterogeneity and multiplicity in the many other possible ways that the stories of women in the dance world may be recovered and re-told, at the same time that it can raise significant critiques and meaningful alternatives to the hegemony of traditional dance history. Feminism and its various interventions as a social movement or a mode of theorizing, after all, are inevitably plural, strategically aligned yet politically fractured. As Pollock (1996a) elaborates:

> Feminism stands for a commitment to the full appreciation of what women inscribe, articulate, voice and image in cultural forms: interventions in the fields of meaning and identity from the place called "woman" or the "feminine." Feminism also refers to a theoretical revolution in the ways in which terms such as art, culture, woman, subjectivity, politics and so forth are understood. *But feminism does not imply a unified field of theory, political position or perspective. Feminism has been identified with a women's movement and it is important historically that it should be so.* (1996, xv; italics mine)

These significant threads of clues that unveiled through my research process signal how small dissident voices can touch others to move in similar gestures of defiance, transgressing through limits and gaps in generations or geographies where these thinking and theorizing may spring from.

And so it is not that I venture unquestioningly in embracing the paradigms of largely Euro-American feminists, from which these frames mostly come. But that in re-configuring these perspectives in my own space and context in the Third World as a young feminist academic, I remain self-reflexive and self-aware in my critical approach of a contextual and materialist reading of this/these self/selves that are re-presented and re-inscribed in these narratives.

This writing in a sense ceases to become a mere scholarly project of one isolated academic thinker and researcher, as I share this text as a site of solidarity with other communities of thinkers, dancers, and movers in contemporary culture. This, in a sense, becomes a collaborative project invoking three local women dance artists—thinkers and important cultural and social movers in their own right—who share here their stories of difference and dissidence within a dominant Philippine dance world that is structured by colonial and androcentric constructs and canons.

But this is not to simplistically valorize or celebrate the women in this study as a "chosen few artists" with success stories to brandish for making it into an equally elitist canon of Philippine dance history. I propose that the three Filipina women dancing independently cannot be viewed in a single monolithic manner. They were chosen here not so their status in the dance world would be canonized, but because of the consistency of their engagements in the dance world and the clarity of their articulated vision. Independent dancing by women does not constitute a singular dancing self but is inflected by the various and shifting scripts of identity and context.

This project aims to critically and politically situate the presence of women in dance and lay bare their valuation of being independent artists, thus situating the very subjectivities of their selves with their historical and material determinations as constituted by class, race, ethnicity, nationality, gender and other identifications in an asymmetrical landscape of shifting social powers.

With this project then, I aim to critically re-inscribe the voices of three women dance artists and re-articulate their presence in the history of Philippine contemporary dance. It is a critical testimony, a mediated witnessing, as their voices I re-inscribe here would historicize specific bodies that gesture into specific movements—the personal and the political, the individual and the social—each one articulating her own version of an aesthetic of independence in her own context in Philippine society and the dance world. This in turn would lay bare the politics of power vested in dance as a significantly lived and living experience of women who attempt to work within and beyond dominant traditions of society and culture through their dance practice and aesthetic. It is their specific narratives, together with ours, that I have chosen to re-tell here.

Thus, these are the stories of three women in independent dance.

Historicizing Women and Independent Dancing

This book is necessarily historical, informed by certain theoretical frames, and not a mere journalistic account of atheoretical impressions about three women in dance. I find that it is equally vital for dance scholars as much as for feminist researchers to be familiar with the theories and categories laid out here, not so much because I propose that these are the only tools of analyses that can be used in reading dance, but simply because I would like to present here *another* way of reading dance other than the popular notion of its being a mere "entertainment art," one that does not merit rigorous academic discussion and discourse. In engaging here a feminist criticism and historicizing of dance, I would like to consciously veer away from the idea that dance deserves only a few columns of impressionistic descriptions in the lifestyle section of a newspaper; or worse, that the notion of dance, like any other art form, is gender-less and completely devoid of social, racial, and class influence. For these reasons, I feel compelled to do no less than to lay bare here the trajectory of my narrative via chapters that build up on theoretical concepts and a framework of a feminist historiography of dance, properly placed within the frame of Philippine and general dance history.

Chapter 1 opens up the setting of dance in Western intellectual thought and the place of women within this worldview. It also takes notice of the various disciplinal and discursive routes that this research has set to navigate. Chapter 2 outlines the critical categories of feminist dance histories that make up my framework and its accompanying research methodologies, detailing the rigorous but necessary questionnaire which leads us to a well-informed historicizing of the three women in dance. I offer a general context of Philippine dance history in chapter 3, giving an overview of women's roles in Philippine ballet, modern and contemporary dance movements. This logically leads to chapter 4 where we find the specific articulations of Myra Beltran, Kristin Jackson, and Agnes Locsin. In chapters 5, 6, and 7, I synthesize the results of the previous chapters' assertions and analyze the recurring patterns and issues on the identity of independent dancing as practiced by the three women. I reflect on the challenges encountered in the research process, ponder on future possibilities of independent dancing and feminist research of dance, and finally, I conclude with personal reflections on how this project in itself is an independent performance replete with notions of defiance in a largely untended domain of women's history in dance.

CHAPTER 1

Women and Dance in Society

Dance is the sole art where the whole human body communicates while moving through patterns of time, sound, and space. But it is precisely because of this centrality given to the body that dance has been considered a marginal art form. Western dualisms have viewed the body as inferior to mind and soul, which explains the present-day idea of "mind over matter" and the religious platitude that "the spirit is willing but the flesh is weak."

Feminist theologian Felicity Edwards would trace the evolution of the dualist thought in pre-classical and ancient Hebrew society: the human person holistically; later, "as Orphic influence impinged on classical thought, the human person came to be viewed dualistically as made up not so much of complementary, but rather mutually opposed elements: body and mind" (Edwards 1995, 180). She further explains the serious implications of this bifurcation of being in relation to gender politics:

> [W]hen the body/mind dualism became assimilated to the already existing female/male dualism of the classical world, the repercussions for women were disastrous and far-reaching. Women came to be identified with matter, the body and sensuality, while the association of the male was the spirit, mind and purity .... Christian missionaries spread it to the colonies of the Western empires and it is still part of our worldview today, charged as it is with harmful attitudes that accompany the perceptions of superiority and inferiority. (Ibid)

Western phallogocentric reason brings us to a host of other mutually exclusive polarities engendered by the basic mind/body opposition—reason/passion, light/dark, culture/nature, One/other, masculine/feminine, and even the Orientalist West/East dichotomy as Edward Said theorized. Man was thus aligned with the first superior side, and woman with the other negative opposition. This logic corresponds to the imperialist and patriarchal civilizing mission of the white, Christian, heterosexual male to explore and subjugate his *others.*

Such conquest-driven thinking is particularly apparent in the dances in most Western cultures. For instance, ballet—which had its heyday in French, Italian, and English courts of the sixteenth to seventeenth centuries, and later in nineteenth to twentieth century Tsarist Russia—was appropriated by the European aristocracy from the dances of the peasant and working classes of Europe to form a codified and highly stylized dance spectacle where the female dancers were idealized as sylphs and virginal muses (Adair 1992, 118).

Classical ballet technique, whose five basic positions of the feet are attributed to French nobleman and choreographer Pierre Beauchamp, requires the perfect line of the dancer's physique (Funk and Wagnalls 1993, 221). This stress given on verticality and symmetry was influenced by the classical Greco-Roman idealization of the human body, physically evident in ballet's repertoire of anti-gravitational steps of elevation and flight. Examples of these are the grand jete (big jump) and multiple leaps of the danseur, and the ballerina's reserved, mincing bourrees while in her restricting *pointe* shoes. These movements that repudiate gravity come from an anti-body philosophy which seeks to discipline the flesh towards the achievement of an ethereal, immortal, and celestial ideal.

Dance has thus been alienated from the working classes, while its status as art declined due to the Christian church fathers' restriction of the body. The spiritual shackle on the body was further confounded by the economic prerequisites brought about by the advent of the Industrial Revolution. This ensured the use of the body for economic production: the body/mind split was very much in accord with the values of the then emerging capitalist society, whose main ethic was "the selling of one's body to another for the purpose of making profit (surplus value)" (Goodman in Hanna 1988b, 124). This is particularly true in ballet history when the term "ballet girl"—which derogatorily connoted being a prostitute of a wealthy male audience—surfaced in the mid-twentieth century (Ibid). Logically, the existing economic, social, and religious hegemony of Western culture and society supported the patriarchal dualist reasoning, which became responsible for the nearly parallel marginality conferred to women and dance in society.

In contrast to the aforementioned repulsive attitudes toward women and the dancing body are the earthbound dance practices of African and Asian societies where dance is an intimate part of the indigenous people's everyday life. Dance for them is a communal and ritualistic activity that marks the passage of significant life occurrences such as birth, courtship, marriage, battle, and death. As Alice Guillermo posits:

> The social values that ... indigenous and traditional dances convey are ... markedly different from those of the Western world. While in the latter context, dances function mainly to create an artistic form of erotic play, or to suggest transcendental concepts of ethereality and spiritual flight from the world as physical and hence gross, here the indigenous Asian dances are imbued with a social and ceremonial character because of their ritualistic origins. The dancer continues the tradition of the *babaylan* or priestess, intermediary between man and the spirits of nature. (Guillermo 1988, 114)

The perceived matriarchy of pre-colonial Philippines is not yet an established fact in the academe, but there is at least a basic notion that women were regarded highly during those times. But with the onset of the Western imperialist mission, cultural aggression invaded the native lands and weakened most of the rites and their concomitant indigenous values and practices. Enduring "three hundred years of convent and fifty years of Hollywood," the Philippines in particular is heir to a colonial tradition that has effectively disposed the locals with so many misogynist values and practices surrounding the body, especially the female body. This manifested when ballet first made its way into the country via the American colonizers: moral guardians from the Catholic Church imposed a "ballet ban," prohibiting students from taking classes in ballet, which they deemed "immoral" (Alejandro 1978, 57).

Dance has thus been made a marginal study in the field of art and cultural studies, and hardly considered worthy of serious academic scholarship. It has been relegated to the non-rational realm in Western academic thinking that privileges the mind over the body, reason over emotion, masculine over feminine, and other similar phallogocentric "One"-over-the-"other" dualisms.

This marginal status of dance as an art form is particularly seen in the dispersal and subsumption of dance under the regime of various colleges and departments, particularly in the University of the Philippines. The UP College of Music used to offer only a diploma course in dance, and, recently, a bachelor of music degree in dance; under the College of Human Kinetics, dance is one among many other physical education subjects; and in the College of Arts and Letters' Department of Art Studies, dance is taught as two rarely offered elective courses in a semester.

Women, however, have historically played an important role in the dance world as they have dominated the field as dancers and choreographers, vested with the powers to perform, create, and produce dances. A large number of women in Philippine theatrical and concert dance have progressively gone beyond the role of being dancers and have become dance educators, choreographers, and artistic directors as they have matured in their careers. But despite the predominance of women in the field, the discipline perpetuated by the traditional agents of dance continue to carry some of the traditional notions and hierarchies about what a "great dance" or a "great dancer" is, among other crucial notions embedded in dance practices in the ballet schools and dance companies.

It is in this light that three independent women dancers have, in contemporary times, attempted to trail-blaze with small attempts at dance-making within and outside the hegemonic mold of the ballet school tradition and the dance company system. All women dancers in this study have received their formative training under the auspices of these two traditional agencies and have also decided to move away from them at critical periods in their dancing lives. Each has made her own space outside these dominant traditions with the attempt of creating new meanings, new images, and imaginings of what dancing is and could be in her self-defined site and context.

Disciplinal and Discursive Contexts

This book straddles several disciplinal and discursive lines that are strategically interwoven to properly contextualize the largely unaccounted for scholarship in Philippine dance history, especially in the light of well-placed canons of art history.

The first backdrop is provided by the contexts of *art history* and *dance history*, both distinctive fields of study that developed largely in the Western academe. Art history, which mainly started and developed in Continental and North American countries (Datuin 2002, 31), is a mode of historical inquiry of art that largely deals with the history of visual arts—its artists, their texts and contexts, together with an analysis of the modes of artistic production and consumption, and the various methods of recounting and disseminating the story of art (Preziosi in Datuin 2002, 31).

Dance history has also largely been developed in the West, and mainly centered on the historical perspectives on dance by the white aristocracy (Adair 1992, 7; Villaruz 1999, 87). It has traditionally borrowed from other disciplines such as anthropology and musicology. However, dance history also includes the mythologizing and highly romanticized reviews, articles, and books on "star dancers" and "star choreographers" that do not situate dance within its broader socio-cultural contexts (Carter 1998). Locally, dance history in the form of research and documentation of Philippine folk and regional dances has been notably practiced since the 1930s as pioneered by Francisco Reyes Tolentino; in the 1960s by Libertad Fajardo; in the 1950s to the 1960s by Lucrecia Reyes-Urtula, Lucresia Kasilag, Isabel Santos; and in the 1980s by Ligaya Amilbangsa, among others. The journalistic and literary type of dance criticism was locally practiced by Leonor Orosa Goquingco and Anita Kane in the 1960s; by Isabel Taylor, Josephine Acosta, and Elizabeth Reyes in the 1970s; and from the 1960s to present by Basilio Esteban Villaruz, and intermittently by Marge Enriquez in the 1980s. Much of Philippine dance criticism has been descriptive and romanticized, and "has not gone beyond what it was in the 1960s and 70s" (CCP Encyclopedia of Philippine Art 1994, 120). Local dance historical practice has for the most part been reduced to the esoteric and highbrow—such as the production of coffee-table books, or hagiographic accounts of so-called "great dancers" (Corpus 1996, 8)—and often relegated to the aristocratic discourse of high-society pages (Datuin 1999, 130).

Only in the past two decades has dance scholarship and historiography developed as an autonomous and critical academic discipline in the West. It can be categorized as follows: *dance history and criticism*, which evaluate dance based on aesthetic judgment; and *dance ethnology/anthropology*, which are concerned with the chronicling of the wider cultural functions of dance. The former disciplines are mostly associated with the study of Western dance forms, while the latter with the non-Western dances (Grauer in Jonas 1992). One example of Philippine dance ethnographic writing is *Body, Movement, and Culture: Kinesthetic and Visual Symbolism in a Philippine Community* (1992)—an ethnographic study of the Sinulog dance tradition of Cebu City—by Sally Ann Ness.

The second discursive context is *feminist art history* and *feminist dance histories*. Thrust by Linda Nochlin's seminal essay "Why have there been no great women artists?" in the 1970s, the two are relatively young and emergent disciplines, using feminist paradigms to criticize the entrenched canons of traditional art- and dance history. Both have yet to find their own development in Asian and Philippine academes.

Taking on the trajectories of largely Euro-American feminisms, feminist art history in the country has been taught and incorporated by some teachers at the UP Department of Art Studies in their art history/

criticism courses. Two of its primary practitioners in the department, and in the country, are Professors May Datuin, especially in her dissertation and book *Home Body Memory: Filipina Artists in the Visual Arts, 19th Century to the Present* (2002), and Eloisa May Hernandez, in her thesis and book *Homebound: Women Visual Artists in Nineteenth Century Philippines* (2004). Both works tackle women in Philippine visual art history using feminist art-historical approaches.

Feminist dance histories, meantime, is practically unknown and non-existent as a mode of discourse in local academia. There are however intermittent attempts to use feminist paradigms in understanding dance: May Datuin's essay "Beyond the Coffee-Table: Toward a Feminist Understanding of Dance" (1999); the author's own undergraduate thesis on a feminist reading of dance, "Reading Mariang Sinderela" (1996 and 1999); and other critical academic papers by the author on topics surrounding the critical constructs on feminism, women, the dancing body, and dance (Corpus 1999; 2000; 2003; 2004 a and c). In the compilation of works titled *1998 Philippine International Dance Conference*, significant efforts at a gendered reading of dance were essayed by Ruby Palma Beltran in "Dance as Gender and Empowerment Issue," and Ricardo Trimillos in "Gender in Dance Performance: Constructions and Paradigms from the Asia-Pacific Region." Roselle Pineda in the same collection tackled the gendered performativity of lesbian issues in dance in "Out of the Closet, Into the Dance: Performing Lesbian Eroticism through Dance." Basilio Villaruz likewise offered an essay called "Skirting an Issue," which confronted the gendered stereotypes about men in the dance world. Contemporary dancer Myra Beltran tells her idea of the body in "Reclaiming the Body as Home: A Rite of Passage to the 21st Century." All these attempts, however, are hardly recognized in the Philippine academe as distinct and significant contributions towards a fledgling discipline called feminist dance histories.

Women and Dance in Various Texts and Contexts

With the dearth of local critical and scholarly production on women dancers, I draw mainly from Euro-American writings centering on topics such as women artists, dance history, feminist art history, feminist research methodologies, and other critical readings on women in the art world. For the past two decades, Euro-American academia has developed a growing number of feminist scholarships in cultural studies and dance studies, engaging issues such as space, the body, power, and gender politics in dance. This set of materials proved to be useful in providing perspectives and a contextual backdrop to the project at hand.

Locally, the largely descriptive accounts found in local publications on dance—such as the coffee-table books of Reynaldo Alejandro (*Philippine Dance*, 1978; *Sayaw*, 2002) and hagiographic biographies by Nick Joaquin (*La Orosa*, 1994)—seem to construe Philippine dance history as a mere listing of personages and chronicles of picture-perfect moments in its history. So far, the volume on Philippine Dance in the *CCP Encyclopedia of Philippine Art* (1994) offers the most useful and comprehensive written history of Philippine dance.

It is around six thematic clusters that I mobilize the literature used and are related to this study: a) general art history; b) Philippine dance history; c) general dance studies d) feminist art history; e) feminist dance histories; and f) feminist research methodologies.

General art history

Eric Ferne's *Art History and Its Methods* (1995) tackles the various art historical methods from antiquity to contemporary times. It is useful in its comprehensive presentation as a study of art historical methods by offering a collection of excerpted writings of various art historians. Each excerpted essay is accompanied by an introduction about the author's life and work, a summary of the essay's mains points, and a brief analytical commentary from Ferne. It also includes a glossary of concepts used in the book. The anthology offers a comprehensive specialist grounding on Western art history, with informed and evaluative commentaries from the author.

Philippine dance history

The *CCP Encyclopedia of Philippine Art, Volume 5* is focused on Philippine dance history from pre-colonial to contemporary times. At the end of the volume is a collection of brief bio-notes which lists significant groups and personages in Philippine dance. The short biographies of two of the dance artists under study here, Agnes Locsin and Kristin Jackson, are found in this attempt at a canonical listing.

The coffee-table books of Reynaldo Alejandro, *Philippine Dance* (1978) and *Sayaw* (2002) offer glossy full-page pictures of various dance traditions in the country. These are useful pictorial references in looking at the visual imagery of dances, despite the largely impressionistic and descriptive method of its writing.

The Dances of the Emerald Isles (1980) by Leonor Orosa Goquingco is a richly colored collection of photographs of dances and a chronicle of the dance traditions of the Philippines, from those of indigenous communities, Muslims, and Christianized Filipinos.

Subli: Isang Sayaw sa Apat na Tinig (1989) by Elena Mirano is a chronicling of the subli religious folk dance tradition in Batangas. The book foregrounds the subli performers, the historical records on subli, the poetry/dance/musical texts of the subli, and the researcher's observations of the dance tradition.

The World Dance Alliance Conference Book titled *1998 Philippine International Dance Conference* (1999) edited by Philippine dance scholar Professor Basilio Esteban Villaruz from the University of the Philippines offers a diverse collection of essays on dance read and presented in the aforesaid event. Among the more useful essays in this research were those of Myra Beltran—"Reclaiming the Body as Home," which tackles the ritualistic roots of Philippine contemporary dance—and Agnes Locsin—"Transformation of Aboriginal Movement into Contemporary Choreography," which is about her choreographic process in transforming indigenous movements into contemporary dance works. Others of use here are Villaruz's "Who Writes Dance History?" which critiques the Western-centered history of the dance world, and May Datuin's "Beyond the Coffee-Table: Toward a Feminist Understanding of Dance" which poses possible critical categories in looking at dance.

General critical dance studies

Dance, Modernity and Culture by Helen Thomas is the first attempt at a sociological approach to dance. Specifically studying American modern dance, it looks at gender and women's social roles in the dance form.

June Layson and Janet Adshead-Lansdale's *Dance History: An Introduction* (1994) is a collection of essays about methods on studying and writing dance history. It is mostly contextualized in looking at European dance traditions.

The Routledge Dance Studies Reader (1998), edited by Alexandra Carter, is an anthology of essays by European and American dancers, choreographers, dance critics, and scholars from the 1980s and 1990s. The collected works address issues on choreographing, performing, writing criticism, studying dance, dance in history and society, and analysis of dance works.

Dancing: The Pleasure, Power, and Art of Movement (1998) by Gerald Jonas is a general reference and picture book capturing various dance cultural traditions in the world. More than a mere encyclopedic and generalist account of dances, it approaches dance along specific thematic lines: dance as cultural identity; as religious worship; as expression of social order, power and cultural mores; as classical art; as medium of cultural fusion; as creation of individual artists; and, as indicator of contemporary identity.

Sally Ann Ness' "Originality in the Postcolony: Choreographing the Neoethnic Body of Philippine Ballet" is a critical engagement of Agnes Locsin's neo-ethnic ballet *Igorot*, mobilizing its various constructions around nationhood, ethnicity, aesthetics, and culture.

Feminist art history

Excerpts of Griselda Pollock's "Feminist Interventions in the Histories of Art" in Ferne's anthology *Art History and its Methods* is useful in its mapping of the political positionings of feminist discourse in art history. Pollock's *Generations and Geographies*, for its part, is a critical anthology of various artists' and writers' essays tackling feminist readings of art; it aims to break down barriers between feminist art practice and theorizing. However, it is wholly focused on the visual arts as source of text and art works.

Astri Wright's *"Self-Taught All the Way: Three Contemporary Women Artists in Indonesia"* (1999a) is a non-traditional, self-reflexive art historical narrative of three Indonesian women artists and the writer herself, whose experiences intersect as self-taught women in their fields (visual arts and research, respectively). Feminist and liberationist pedagogies are effectively advocated as mode and method of study and re-writing the *othered* subjects in the masculinist and colonial art history.

May Datuin's book *Home Body Memory: Filipina Artists in the Visual Arts, 19th Century to the Present* (2002) is a critical feminist historical study of women artists in the Philippine visual arts from the nineteenth century to contemporary times. Datuin discusses the use of feminist discourse in looking at the "feminine elsewhere"—as used by Pollock and de Lauretis—which becomes her mode of analyzing the works of women and the idea of "the feminine" in the study.

Feminist dance histories

Women and Dance: Sylphs and Sirens (1992) by Christy Adair looks at the history of Western theatrical dance, modern and postmodern styles, and the various roles, representations and resistances of women in the Western dance world. Hers is a materialist-feminist approach, looking at dance along lines of gender, race, sex, and ethnicity, among other context-specific identities.

"Re-tracing our steps: The possibilities for feminist dance histories" by Carol Brown in the aforementioned anthology *Dance History: An Introduction* (1994) is a progressive attempt at looking at the key connections of dance and feminism, using the female body and its constructions as space of inquiry. Brown's proposed critical approaches to writing feminist dance histories are largely resonated in this study.

Sally Banes' *Dancing Women: Female Bodies on Stage* (1998) retells the story of Western theatrical dancing from the romantic ballets to modern dance by probing the construction of women and female identity in the dances of the Western dance canon. Taking on a hermeneutic approach, it treats dance performances—rather than plots—as main texts, as indices of underlying power relations. It is in this sense a contribution to the field of feminist dance histories and criticism.

Anna Aalten's "Performing the Body, Creating Culture" in the book *Embodied Practices: Feminist Perspectives on the Body* (1997, edited by Kathy Davis) is a first-person critical account of her experience, as dance researcher and former dancer, on the female body in Western ballet tradition. She studies the body as a historical conscription and surfaces the disempowering and empowering practices in ballet training for women and men.

Moving Words: Rewriting Dance (1996) by Gay Morris is a collection of essays discussing critical ways of looking at dance. One of its more useful essays is Leslie Satin's "Being Danced Again: Reclaiming the Girlchild," which reads Meredith Monk's dance *Education of a Girlchild* within the frame of women's autobiographical narrative in dance-form.

Edited by Sherry Shapiro, *Dance, Power and Difference: Critical and Feminist Perspectives on Dance Education* (1998) is a collection of essays by dance educators, scholars, and dancers from the US, England, Canada, New Zealand and Brazil that use critical and postmodern theories on teaching, researching and practicing dance. Autobiographical reflections by Shapiro and contributors are helpful in integrating the interface of the personal and the political issues of teaching and practicing dance, and its empowering possibilities in various cultural contexts.

Feminist research methodologies

Gender Sensitive and Feminist Methodologies: A Handbook for Health and Social Researchers (2002), edited by Sylvia Guerrero, is an anthology of essays that offer gender-sensitive, participatory, and feminist methodologies in the field, especially in the Philippine social context.

Brown's "Re-tracing our Steps" and Wright's "Self-Taught All the Way" similarly offer feminist methodologies.

In sum, Philippine scholarship on dance has remained small and marginal, descriptive and atheoretical, in contrast to the more developed scholarship and literature on the visual arts. Locally, there have been recent intermittent attempts at dance criticism and a gender analysis of dance. In the West, however, there are already a number of pioneering essays and books connecting gender and dance studies, and even feminist politics with dance. Consolidated, these materials provide a general backdrop for a contextual study of dance, mobilizing critical and feminist approaches to the subject of women dance artists in Philippine contemporary dance.

CHAPTER 2

Defying and Defining: Feminist Dance Histories of Independent Women Dance-Makers

Part of the project of performing feminist dance histories is to illustrate the conceptual categories and ideological constructs that constitute the horizon of this dance historical writing. This chapter outlines the perspectives embedded in these key categories, and the intellectual lineage from which they have sprung.

Feminist Dance Histories as an/Other Narratives

Feminisms are a polyvalent mode of discursive practice rupturing patriarchal traditions, and whose critical tools of analysis I primarily appropriate in this rewriting of histories of women in dance and art history. History as a traditionally male domain has silenced women's participation in the very writing of its story. The discipline of art history is also influenced by the masculinist bias upholding men as the sole and natural creator of art and its narratives. This dominant construction in Western epistemologies pervades intellectual and academic disciplines—such as history, sociology, political science, anthropology, art- and dance history—in the way that they homogenize knowledge that is defined by the white Christian bourgeois male. Feminists have criticized Western knowledge, which operates within a dichotomy of subject vs. object, and wherein "male/masculine subjects" are privileged to observe and peruse "female/feminine objects," therefore erasing the agency of women as knowers. This is seen particularly in the history of dance writing in the West: it was largely men who wrote dance literature until the mid-twentieth century, and in a style that often objectified the dancer, usually female, as "an object of beauty and desire" (Brown 1994, 199).

The canonical term "History" in this writing is deliberately pluralized into histories, a way of shattering the singularity and dominance of the male voice in traditional historical writing. As a term, histories is also a way of unveiling the voices and selves in these multiple layering of stories, including my own as author. Histories as defined here reconstructs the asymmetrical relations/positions constitutive of Western androcentric epistemologies: it signals both presence and power of women as legitimate agents of art, dance, and the writing of its histories. These histories or stories are decidedly feminist: they are aligned towards reinscribing the effaced voices of women.

It is in this context of retelling the stories of women dance-makers that I appropriate the aforesaid ideologemes via the term feminist dance histories, a recent and emergent category developed mainly in the seminal writings of independent dancer and dance scholar Carol Brown.

In her essay, "Re-tracing our steps: the possibilities for feminist dance histories" in the anthology *Dance History: An Introduction* (1994), Brown outlines the potential feminist strategies in historicizing women in the dance world amidst the largely androcentric writing of dance history—one which is characteristically anecdotal and atheoretical, and has idealized the "Woman" as the passive muse-dancer to the active creator-genius who is the male choreographer. Brown cites Christy Adair's *Women and Dance* (1992) as one of the first examples of feminist dance historical writing in Britain that engaged the tropes of feminism and dance in rereading the diverse and critical histories of women in Western theatrical dancing, particularly in ballet and modern dance.

In her essay, Brown comprehensively suggests several ways of writing history informed by feminist paradigms in research and writing. They are summarized as follows:

a. Decoding images of women by mobilizing the issue of representation of the female body in dance;
b. Appraisal of the dancing foremothers by chronicling achievements of women in the dance world;
c. Materialist approaches to dance history—modes of production, distribution and reception; and the relationship of dance to other discourses; and
d. Poststructuralist valuations of fragmentary identities and subjectivities in dance and its histories (Brown 1994, 213).

I mobilize in this project these four paths that go against the grain of traditional art/dance history, recognizing too the multiplicity of resistance offered by feminisms as a discourse of shifting strategic maneuvers. I am aware that there could be other ways of writing feminist dance histories that may not yet be conceived on paper. However, I recognize that these are as yet the most potent categories proposed in the field of dance scholarship. These categories draw mainly from the following currents: semiotics, which can potently offer readings of representations of women's images in dance; feminist and women's studies, which recovers the names and re-valuates women's presence in the dance world; Marxist analysis, whose materialist approach looks at dance in its structures of production, consumption, and distribution, and which views the dancing body (usually female) as a social and historical product, not as a mere transcendental essence of femininity; and poststructuralism, which radically disrupts "History" and "Truth" as it marks the fragmentary identities of the self/ author, and values deconstruction as a mode of interrogating conventional history.

And so as I read the dance works of the three women artists in my narratives, I am involved in the project of decoding representations of the female body, which is a strategic site of ideological and material determinations. Secondly, by the very choice and act of writing these narratives of these independent women dance-makers, I summon forth a critical appraisal of the endeavors of three dance-makers in Philippine dance history—a necessary first step in rewriting the shifting presence of women in dance. As a materialist approach to dance, on the other hand, I contextualize herein dance as a material practice within the bounds of the dance-makers' class, gender and racial subjections. Moreover, I make productive use of post-structuralism's radical rupturing of a singular historical voice of "truth" with the method I call women's "story-sharing": it values "experiential knowledge concentrating on traces, such as oral history and autobiography" (Brown 1994, 211), together with my intervention as a self-reflexive mediator. This is another way of posing a deconstructionist critique to the pervasive notion of a detached and value-free historical writing.

It is along these lines that I reconfigure feminist dance histories as a narrative and mode of countering the hegemony of traditional androcentric writing of art and dance history in the Philippines. It is also along this methodological trajectory that I move towards a larger research aim of constructing a theory and aesthetic of independence, both in dance practice and dance historical writing.

Independent Dancing as Dignity and Defiance

Another crucial term is "independent dance practice." It is used here as a category of artistic practice constituted by dance artists who perform and function independent of institutions, usually dominant ones (i.e., dance companies, ballet schools, cultural centers), and who therefore define themselves as an "alternative" to the mainstream of dominant culture. It is in this sense that they are construed to be defying mainstream traditions of androcentric and Western-imposed dance practice. It may also be construed as an assertion of artistic autonomy and dignity in terms of defining one's dance aesthetic and practice—a defiance of the deeply entrenched hierarchical master-apprentice relationship in dance companies and conservatories.

Independent as a term is appropriated in this context to refer to an alternative mode of practicing dance, self-directed and conscious of its departure from the dominant dance and cultural institutions. Independent is, however, a shifting and strategic category that suggests the different and multiple tracks and trajectories that can be taken within dance practice. It is therefore not meant to carve out an exclusivist realm of "women independently dancing" which would tend to create an inverted elitism. The dancers under study show the fluidity and collaborative nature of their relationships with the mainstream of dance and cultural institutions. Independent as a category of cultural practice is therefore under investigation and not turned into a canonical preserve. This study shows the multiplicity of independent dance practice as appropriated and defined by three of its local practitioners in the dance profession.

"Independent dancing" as used here is inflected by the feminist dance historian's stance of chronicling the achievements of women in dance in departing from tradition-bound institutions, in order to reclaim their artistic autonomy and integrity, and also to critically appraise the resistances against—as well as collusions with—the dominant values and practices in the dance world.

Women as Dance Makers/Dance Artists

"Dance-making" as used here is the act of creating dances as a legitimate site and practice of artistic creativity. Women are not considered to be natural creators of art in a male-centered art world, as is presupposed by the oft-used term "female-artist" or "woman-artist." Men on the other hand are always readily conferred the singular canonical title of "the Artist."

Hence, the term "women dance makers" is appropriated here to signify women as active creators of art and dance, as dancers, choreographers or dance teachers/educators. This term will be used interchangeably with "women dance artists" as a mode of demolishing the idea in the canons of Western High Art of the male as the sole author, genius, and creator. This in turn actively puts to question the status quo in Art History "[whose] ... present practices ... not only suppress knowledge of women artists but disallow the very idea of women being 'artists' in the canonical sense of the word. The ideological project of the discourse of art history is to render masculinity and creativity naturally synonymous" (Pollock 1996a, 13).

Likewise, this assignation of women as creators, makers, and artists of dance invalidates the notion of woman as the perpetually passive muse of the male creator, an idea largely present in both literary and visual representations of "woman" in the traditional anecdotal writings embedded in Western dance history.

And so the term "woman" as used here does not refer to a mythologized "universal woman" or signify an idealized "essential feminine/femininity." It is a construct that is always materially and historically determined, therefore shifting in its locations and its histories. There is no one type of "woman": "womanhood" and the "feminine" have multiple historical, personal, and social locations that construct and define "woman" as an always ideology-specific site of identity.

The Body as Site of Power

An aspect significant to the understanding of dance lies in the engagement of the body, and the discourses viewing it as a site of power and contestation. Being the sole art form that uses the body as its main medium of communication by moving through patterns of time, sound and space, dance has been marginally studied in Western masculinist thought, precisely because it accords the body centrality—a privilege the Western binarist scheme bestows upon the mind.

In this project however, the body is remobilized not as a neutral, naturally passive entity, but a cultural agency. The body contains the ideological determinations within the culture and society that shape and condition it in turn. For instance, the classical ballerina's dance movements are not neutral and natural postures; they are the product of years of dance training within a body-control regime towards the achievement of an ideology of beauty as conceived in the European aristocratic aesthetic of symmetry and flexibility of the female form. The body of a ballerina is hence gender- and class-specific, as ballet is a European aristocratic art form codified under the gaze and pleasure of a largely male aristocratic aesthetic and choreography. In the same manner, in the context of Philippine popular culture, the dance movements of the Sex-Bomb Girls are not spontaneous gyrations of naturally outgoing, young, scantily-dressed women. In contrast, they are predisposed by unequal sexual power relations upholding the ideology of patriarchy in its catering to the culturally conditioned "pleasures" of a largely male and macho viewership.

In Western dance history, the dancing body has been largely construed as an ahistorical entity. Moreover, the female body in dance has been mystified as an essential feminine, making it an image of an obsessively idealized femininity that has been enshrined in the writings of mostly male writers, prominently by Theophile Gautier (1811-72), who would generally call themselves "balletomanes" or ballet-goers (Brown 1994, 199).

By being aware of the historicity of the dancing body, the feminist dance historian necessarily fractures such colonization of the body. Judith Butler historicizes the body by seeing it as "an intentionally organized materiality ... always an embodying of possibilities conditioned and circumscribed by historical convention" (Butler in Aalten 1997, 47).

This notion of the body as social, cultural and historical construction would oppose the pervasive idea of understanding the body as merely based on mystified, including biological, essentialisms. It would allow for an understanding of the body as a field of multiple cultural constructions and differences (Adair 1992, 199). This is particularly useful in understanding the body in dance given that the body is the main medium in dance training and practice. The body, when regarded as a "site of social, political, cultural, and geographical inscriptions, production, or constitution" would annul the dualism viewing it as "opposed to culture, a resistant throw-back to a natural past." Feminist philosopher Elizabeth Grosz further discusses this other way of looking at the body:

> The specificity of bodies must be understood in its historical rather than simply its biological concreteness. Indeed, there is no body as such: there are only bodies—male or female, black, brown, white, large or small—and the gradations in between .... There are always only specific types of body, concrete in its determinations, with a particular sex, race, and physiognomy. Where one body (in the West, the white, youthful, able, male body) takes on the function of model or ideal, the human body, for all other types of body, its domination may be undermined through a defiant affirmation of a multiplicity, a field of differences, of other kinds of bodies and subjectivities. (Grosz 1994, 19)

This way of perceiving the body is aligned with the notion of Mabel Todd and Christy Adair's thinking body, and of Susan Leigh Foster's writing body, where the body is an active entity of diverse cultural inscriptions resisting submission and passivity as an other to the One normative male and masculine order. This idea also transcends the bifurcation of Being that posit the body as inert, sinful, irrational, and imperfect, as our fathers in the Judeo-Christian world and Western philosophy would have us think.

The prevalent cultural notion stemming from this gender stereotype is the one inscribed in the idea of "unthinking dancers," which we now forfeit here as we look at dancers as active thinkers and creators behind the production of the dance-text. It is not only the role of the choreographers as creators of dance that merits our valuation, but also that of the dancers as artistic creators in their own right. In abandoning the valorization of the individual choreographer as the sole authority and originator of dance, Brown articulates the recovery of dancers as equally important producers and creators of dance and art in general:

> But dancers are not neutral surfaces awaiting masterly inscriptions, they exist as highly trained and articulate experts of movement who color the choreographic process with their own subjectivities. In relinquishing the hierarchical relation between choreographer and dancer, the process of artistic production can be realigned to consider the inventiveness of the dancer as interpreter and articulator of the "text." (Brown 1994, 209)

This is particularly significant in demolishing the gendered hierarchy of male choreographers who were seen in a more privileged position than female dancers in the earlier period of ballet history. The very nature of dance as constantly in process and in progress as it is created and executed resists the idea of dance being a unitary and contained object. Dance is open for a "fluidity of authorship," especially since it is not possible for "a choreographer to transpose exactly her or his movement on to another body." From passive muses, the dancers should be rightfully regarded as co-authors and collaborators in dance-making. Recently, for example, twentieth century ballerinas in the West have been recognized as important collaborators of their various choreographers: Lynn Seymour with Kenneth Macmillan, Margot Fonteyn with Frederick Ashton, Suzanne Farrell with George Balanchine (Robertson and Hutera in Brown 1994, 212).

Locally, Resil Mojares' article on the Visayan bodies is an initial scholarship on the construction of bodies in a specific Philippine region and culture.

The dancing body, and the dancers and choreographers involved in its production, are seen here to be necessarily situated within their specific social and cultural contexts, and the historical conventions and conditions embedded therein. Understanding the social construction and material determinations of the body, we find greater space to articulate how meanings and significations on the moving and dancing body in society can be deconstructed and reconstructed towards more empowering ends and possibilities.

Transgressing Traditions: Feminist Tools and Methods

The methodology used here is informed by several feminist research methodologies, which offer ways of gathering and organizing information that challenge traditional methods operating within masculinist Western epistemologies. Traditional research specifically entrenches the notion of the researcher as the sole active 'knower' discerning and hovering over a passive research subject. In addition, traditional methods ingrain myths of a value-free and detached scholarship that promotes hierarchical and non-reciprocal relationships between the researcher and the object research. These tendencies are challenged in feminist methodologies' advocacy of a "conscious partiality" in collecting research information. "Conscious partiality" tends to make relationships more equitable by situating the researcher "within the same critical plane as the subject of research," thus revealing the "researcher's own bias and positioning within the terms of analysis ... and becomes part of the research process" (Brown 1994, 201).

Carol Brown further suggests this other mode of writing women in history:

> As a corrective to the asymmetry of traditional historical accounts, feminists advocate women's increased participation both as subject of research and as object of analysis. The latter is coterminous with the appropriation of alternative theories of knowledge that legitimate women as 'knowers,' situating them as agents and therefore subjects within history. (Brown 1994, 200)

Relationships with the three dance artists have been initiated and sustained over time by disclosing my multiple roles and interests as a researcher of dance, dance audience, and ballet dancer studying the dance practices of seasoned dance artists. I made sure that relationships formed with the research subjects were within the idiom of professionalism and solidarity that regarded them as agents and not passive objects of one isolated, short-term academic study. Our story-sharing—in the form of conversations, interviews and correspondences—illuminated the relevant connections that bind their ideas and experiences with my own, and with those other dancers or cultural players we commonly know or share affinities with; it was a complex process that invoked a wider community of dance artists and cultural workers in the process.

Another related feminist methodology employed here is the life story, which is "a record of one's inner life" (Guerrero 2002, 69). This was surfaced in this project by gathering information via a combination of interviews—formal (structured and taped) and informal (conversations and story-sharing)—written correspondences with the artists, and fieldwork in the dance spaces of the dance artists. I ensured that the dance artists were able to share their views and histories in a variety of more inclusive forms such as diaries, letters, articles, photos, memorabilia, and other non-traditional sources of historical "evidence" that match what feminist historian Malou Camagay categorizes as "requisites for writing women's history" (2002, 119). And because their voices are central in this project, I made sure that each artist has at least reviewed the manuscripts of the narratives written about them before they are printed for final presentation. This is in keeping with the values of collaborative efforts and mutual goals upheld in this project, in whose methodologies "difference-respecting, experience-sharing, self-reflexive theoretical perspectives" (Wright 1999b, 130) are embedded.

Given the ephemerality of dance as an art form, the dance scholar is challenged to find systematic ways of collecting and organizing data in the research process. Dance and its practices are often likened to oral history given their transitory and fleeting character as medium of expression. Before the advent of video documentation in contemporary times, writers of dance would have to rely on traces of their memories of the dance performance, supplemented at times by program notes, if they are available. This is made more difficult by the fact that there is very little interest on the study of dance notation, especially in the local dance world. This problem presents the need to systematize one's sources of dance materials.

Part of my research technique in writing the histories of women dance-makers is organizing the sources and materials employed in this project based on dance scholar June Layson's listing of dance source categories, mainly: 1) written; 2) visual; and, 3) sound sources (Layson in Carter 1998, 146). The following table shows my sources in this research utilizing the same categories:

Written	Visual	Sound
• Books and essays on feminist art history, feminist dance histories, women, body and dance • Dance reviews • Program notes and brochures • Correspondence with the dance artists (mainly through email) • Journals, diaries, and memorabilia	• CDs or videotapes of dances • Dance performance (includes choreography and costume) • Architecture (includes dance space and stage design) • Photographs	Oral history: interviews (formal and informal) with dance artists and other relevant agents

Finally, the questionnaire given out to the dance artists was constructed to revolve around four thematic and art-historical categories, which are summarized as follows:

a. Biography – The dance artist's personal history and formative dance training; how that conditioned her artistic inclination, as well as her development as an individual woman within her immediate milieu (family, school, dance/ballet school, and other social structures, and so on).

b. Artistic Practice and Production – This explores the circumstances that mark the dance artist's decision for a dance profession as well as the choices, shifts, and critical turns she made in her profession to explore beyond her traditional formative training. It also takes into account the movement practices, dance styles, and traditions which she would label as "independent."

c. Subjectivity and Intersubjectivity – This implicates the production of the self; how a woman's social subjections (class, gender, age, ethnicity, race, nationality, etc.) intersect with her position in the dance world as dancer, choreographer, and teacher. It also looks into the dance-maker's views on women's roles in dance, ideas on feminist politics and/or women's issues, and any limitation, prejudice, as well as sources of power encountered as a woman artist in dance. This is likewise informed by my own mediation as a self-critical and self-reflexive writer/researcher. My own subjectivities and positionalities are surfaced and woven throughout the writing of the dance artists' histories, hence making possible a productive intersubjective dialogue of our diversely constructed and circumstanced selves.

d. Body of Works – This weaves the threads of three distinct though overlapping modes of making sense of each dance artist's body of works. First is *technology*, or how she imagines her creation and performance of dances in terms of technique, dance style, aesthetic strategies and processes. Second is *mode of interpretation*, or the themes, values, and signification that she dominantly sees in her works. It also entails an inquiry of what works she personally finds most representative of her personal aesthetic and politics in dance. Third is *context*, which covers both personal and social realms, such as personal motives and reasons for dancing and continuing with a dance career, and also the larger network of relationships in the dance/art world she finds herself in (cultural institutions, audience, critics, fellow dance-makers, dancers, and so on).

These thematic categories framed my construction of the research questionnaire, as they did in the general flow of the narratives of the dance artists in this study. These themes and the corresponding questions that arise from them are summarized in this table:

Themes	Questions
Biography	***Initiation into the ballet tradition: Formative years as a dancer*** What was your background and training in dance? Who influenced your early (family, education, group involvements) dance training? What were the circumstances (family, education, group involvements) surrounding your formative years as a dancer? What were your significant experiences in your formative training?
Artistic Practice and Production	***Pursuing dance as career/profession*** At what age and stage in your life did you decide to pursue a career in dance? Who or what influenced you in making this decision? What philosophy, styles, aesthetics was of major influence to you in your dancing? Which people around you inspired and influenced you as a dance artist? What politics or set of ideas about dancing do you particularly subscribe to? ***Independent explorations*** What shifts or turns have you made in your career and style of dance-making? What are the major highlights in your dance career that you felt was a break-away from or affirmation of old dance traditions in terms of aesthetics, style, process, strategies? Do you feel that you are working independently from the established cultural institutions or within their structures? In what ways? What are the benefits of working within institutions? Outside them? Do you feel that you are an "independent" dance-maker? How? Would you use that label for yourself?

Themes	Questions
Subjectivity and Intersubjectivity	***Women in dance and other subjectivities*** Do you feel or think there is a special role that women play in the dance world? What is it, and do you think you also play or have played that role? As a woman, have you experienced any prejudice or limitation as a dancer and choreographer? On the other hand, has it been empowering for you to use dance as a medium? In what ways? Do feminism or women's issues inform any of your works (themes, images, subject, etc.) or your dance practice (relationship with dancers, audience, colleagues, institutions, etc.)? Do you feel you are able to transcend any limits of gender, class, ethnicity in your dance practice? Or do you use your multiple identities (gender, class, ethnicity, race) to inform or ground your works? How? Do you think it is necessary for women to go through ballet training to make them a "good dancer?" Why?
Body of Works	***Body of works*** *Technology*: What are the dominant techniques, styles, aesthetics, processes, strategies you employ in your dance practice (both choreography and performance)? *Mode of interpretation*: What are the images and their signification, themes, and meaning system that you have used in your works? What relevance do you particularly give your works? Were there any social issues you wanted to highlight? Cite three works which you feel is most representative of your aesthetics and politics as a dance artist. *Context*: Personal – What is your main motive for creating dance and continuing with this career path in dance? Do you see other possibilities and career paths opening up for you within or outside dance? Social – What has been the general context surrounding the production of your works? Who are the people and institutions you have worked with as a dancer and choreographer? Who is your audience? Are there issues you are responding to in your works?

CHAPTER 3

Generations and Genealogies: Women in Philippine Ballet and Modern Dance

We now critically locate the history of women in ballet and modern dance in the West, and how this history developed in Philippine theatrical dance mainly via American colonization. Besides strategically mapping out the locus of women in Philippine dance history, this chapter also situates the genealogies of the three independent dance makers in this study within the broader context of women's pioneering roles in ballet and modern dance traditions. It also strives to cover the more contemporary articulations of independent dancing and dance-making in the Philippine dance world, in more recent times.

Women in Ballet History

Ballet is considered the crowning achievement of Western theatrical dance art, and is the most valorized in the hierarchy of Western dance forms (Siegel in Carter 1998, 92). Having developed in the European aristocratic courts from the sixteenth to seventeenth centuries and reaching another height in nineteenth and twentieth century Tsarist Russia, ballet throughout its 400-year history has survived various political structures, from monarchies up to present-day democracies. Often compared in status to the Kabuki dance of Japan, ballet as a similar classical art occupies such a status not simply because it is centuries-old, but because it has been sustained by influential social groups—whether as patrons, performers, or spectators—strongly committed to keep the art form from its demise (Jonas 1992, 128).

Women have played major roles, mainly as dancers in the earlier part of ballet history, and soon after as its teachers and choreographers. Ballet's aesthetic of symmetry and straight classical lines allows for the disciplining of the body into one of flexibility, ease, and grace. Achieving this anti-gravitational aesthetic effaces the strenuous stamina and technique demanded of the dancer, as well as the years of sustained training the dancer endures to develop and maintain her bodily regime.

Men were ballet's early creators and choreographers, and women mainly the dancers who would embody and master its technique as ballerinas. This privileged mastery by women of ballet technique reached its height with the invention of the pointe or toe shoes in the 1830s by one of ballet's first female innovators and choreographers, Maria Taglioni. Toe dancing put the women literally up on their toes and above the crowd, as it remained a female-reserve where the ballerina can exert her technical prowess. It further created the illusion of flight and elevation by allowing the ballerina's body a range of movements and heights impossible with previous footwear. This idealization of the female body in classical ballet, however, is seen to be the product of a male-defined vision of femininity; this is best exemplified in the ballet idiom of the *pas de deux*, or partnering, where the female dancer is posited as dependent on her male counterpart. And so despite the predominance of women in ballet, it was the men who were largely behind its production—as choreographers, ballet masters, musicians, librettists, and critics.

However, ballet's permission of women to enter its field—a freedom never before offered to women in any other profession in nineteenth century Europe—is seen to be one of the more liberating aspects of this dance tradition. Recognizing the duality of ballet as both conservative and emancipatory, dance scholar Gerald Jonas avers:

> Ballet was unique in one way; although its dominant institutions (like those of the other arts and indeed European society in general) were in the hands of men, the stars of the ballet stage were women. In no other nineteenth-century enterprise, artistic or otherwise, did women play so significant a role as they did in classical ballet. Behind the scenes, it is true, men remained in charge. Even the most acclaimed ballerinas, quite literally, danced to the tunes of men. With rare exceptions, men ... set the standards and shaped the images that the dancers embodied onstage and off .... *Nevertheless, dance was one area of public endeavor in nineteenth-century Europe where women's talents were not only prized but idolized. The ballerinas whom audiences cheered were well-rewarded; they had both money and fame. They had no reason to separate themselves from the institutions and traditions that had nurtured them.* (Jonas 1992, 191; italics mine)

At a time when women were restricted from the public sphere and mainly confined to the privacy of home and motherhood, ballet offered an alternative to what women have been socialized and expected to do in European society. The popular figure of the ballerina thus became a symbol of freedom, which was erstwhile unknown to the traditional European "lady":

> In an age when most women were trapped in the home as wives and mothers, the "liberated" figure of the ballerina reflects both her unusual physical freedom and also the fact of her dubious social position. It was commonplace that dances were not "respectable," yet nevertheless their popularity was intense. Their image was to be found in prints, in porcelain: the name of the Sylphide advertised parasols; stage coaches were called after dancers; the ballerinas were feted wherever they went. Even Queen Victoria doted upon the ballet. (Clark and Crisp in Sayers 1997, 140)

When ballet reached the Philippines, it was still women who dominated the art form, and their influence continued up to contemporary times. The first ballets in the Philippines came via the American *bodabil* (or vaudeville) stage in 1901. A troupe of ballet dancers from Australia called the *Lilliputians* danced at the Zorilla in 1901. Other foreign performers followed suit, among them the celebrated ballerina Anna Pavlova who danced at the Manila Grand Opera House as part of her 1922 global tour. Anita Kane of New Zealand was one of the first ballet teachers who set up a graded system in ballet education in the country and trained well-established dancers such as Felicitas Layag-Radaic, Julie Borromeo, Effie Nanas, Ester Rimpos, Kristin Jackson, El Gabriel, Tony Llacer, Luis Layag, among others. Notably, Kane created the first Filipino-inspired full-length ballet *Mariang Makiling* (1939) followed by others such as *Mutya ng Dagat* (1958), *Inulan sa Pista* (1961), *Mah Jong* (1962) and *Aswang* (1969). (CCP Encyclopedia 1994, 49)

Luva Adameit, a graduate of the Malinovsky School of Ballet and Free Art in Kiev, Russia also set-up her ballet school in the country in 1927 while teaching at the Philippine Women's University. Adameit trained the first generation of ballet dancers, teachers, and choreographers in the

Philippines, mainly, Leonor Orosa Goquingco, Inday Gaston-Mañosa, Pacita Madrigal, and Remedios de Oteyza. Adameit began the seeds of folkloric theater by staging folk dances such as the Cariñosa and Planting Rice on pointes.

This would influence her students to go into similar projects in dance later on, particularly Orosa-Goquingco who created stylized and Filipinized ballets as *Trend: Return to Native* (1941) and *Filipinescas: Philippine Life, Legend and Lore in Dance* (1961). De Oteyza became known for abstractionist ballets—owing to her training with neo-classical ballet master George Balanchine—which she carried on in setting up her Manila Ballet Company (later known as Hariraya Ballet). Madrigal, meanwhile, collaborated with American couple Ricardo and Roberta Cassell who professionalized dance with their Cassell Dance Studio in 1952. The Cassells, however, left the country in 1956 after the Catholic Church banned ballet in 1955, deeming it "immoral"(Alejandro 1978, 57; CCP Encyclopedia 1994, 50-51).

With liberal democracy endorsed by the American colonial regime, dance flourished. From the late 1940s up to the '60s, foreign dance companies of ballet, folkloric, Spanish, and modern dance styles visited more regularly to perform in the country. Improved air transport and communication systems in the 60s facilitated the influx of American, British, and European ballet teachers and choreographers, and the overseas study of several local dancers as well. Those who remained here continued professionalizing ballet and saw the establishment of ballet companies: Hariraya Ballet and Dance Theater Philippines in 1968, Dance Concert Company in the 1970s, Alice Reyes Modern Dance Company in 1970 (later known as Ballet Philippines), and Ballet Federation of the Philippines in the mid-'70s. In 1987, seeing the artistic spaces opening after the EDSA uprising, directors of these various dance companies and several known gatekeepers of dance—such as National Artist for Dance Orosa-Goquingco, Felicitas Radaic, Julie Borromeo, Eddie Elejar, Tony Fabella, Vella Damian, and Inday Mañosa—gathered to form the Philippine Ballet Theater (PBT). Former Dance Concert Company dancers Shirley Halili-Cruz and Zenaida Halili, formed Quezon City Ballet in 1986. Russian-trained Lisa Macuja, meanwhile, danced with PBT for a time before she opened her own Ballet Manila in 1995, where she is currently artistic director and premiere danseuse. In the field of dance and ballet education, Felicitas Radaic—with co-authors Noordin Jumalon, and Vella Damian—conceptualized and developed the nationally implemented eight-year ballet curriculum called the Philippine Ballet Syllabus. Radaic is known for bringing and practicing the London-based Royal Academy of Dancing syllabus in the country for the past thirty years, and conceptualizing the aforesaid Philippine Ballet Syllabus, now being implemented throughout the country, and recently adopted in Barcelona, Spain.

Since the 1990s, ballet is said to command transnational pride and prestige, with ballet companies thriving in the First World to Third World nations. In Asia, ballet companies receive state support in China, Japan, Korea, Singapore, but sad to say, minimum support in the Philippines. Sally Ann Ness argues that classical ballet has indeed become a medium for projecting certain national and nationalist desires of present-day nation-states.

> Given ballet's global popularity and prestige, the art form is an ideal vehicle for objectifications of nationalist identity that seek to achieve approval and affirmation at international and cosmopolitan venues .... The dancing bodies of national ballet companies are not simply metaphors for a nationalistic fantasy

> but are, in fact, living proof of the "advances" made by individual citizens inhabiting the nation-state. In this respect, dancing bodies are made the sites of nationalism and ballet technique an agent of national reform and progress (1997, 98).

Currently, Philippine Ballet Theater, Ballet Philippines, and Ballet Manila are the country's more renowned professional dance companies, all of which have largely developed under the helm of women as artistic directors, choreographers, teachers and dancers. This open partiality to women, however, does not indicate a more progressive order of things, as these dance companies still perpetuate the same institutional traditions, hierarchies and conservative values around femininity and gender roles that ballet is known to uphold. But owing to exposure to the modern dance idiom, certain companies are gradually breaking down some of ballet's more well-entrenched elitisms. This is most especially seen in the current practice of including modern dance in the regular ballet curriculum, though it may likewise be understood as a cooptation of modern dance's revolutionary principles.

Modern Movers

The revolution in dance that was to be known as "modern dance" in twentieth century America developed as a rebellion for freedom from the tenacious traditions of the ballet aesthetic. Significantly, it was women who singularly pioneered this counter-aesthetic that went against the idealization of femininity epitomized by the ballerina and systems that produced this conservative ideal around her. Bra-less, corset-less, and shoe-less, the founding mothers of the modern idiom performed outside the large institutions that supported ballet. Indeed, modern dance came not from women trained within the ballet establishment, but from the margins of what was legitimately considered the "high art of dance." And so modern dance would trace its development

> from women who set up shop, on their own, as self-proclaimed artists; their goal was unfettered self-expression through body movement. The freedom they won for themselves has invigorated theatrical dance in the West, including ballet, ever since. The women who created modern dance were asserting for themselves something that poets and painters in the West had come to take for granted by the end of the nineteenth century: the right to follow personal inspiration without catering to the tastes of some private or institutional patron. (Jonas 1992, 191).

One of the first to gain recognition in taking on the idiom of modern dance was Loie Fuller of Illinois. She was known for her technical wizardry in creating a serpentine style by dancing with fabrics to create dramatic evocations to the tune of Wagner. In 1892, Loie stirred the audience of Folies-Bergere in Paris with her serpentine dance, and she soon gained admirers among known poets (Mallarme, Yeats), painters (Toulouse-Lautrec, Whistler), and scientists (Pierre and Marie Curie). Jonas' description of Fuller's style brings us close to how the beginning of a historic shift in the dance world stirred other women in America and elsewhere to dance in other ways. Fuller is thus recognized,

> in her ability to epitomize the taste of an entire generation, she was a successor of the Taglionis and Elsslers of the earlier nineteenth century. But unlike those ballerinas, whose careers had been formed within a long established artistic tradition, Fuller was a self-made artist who ran her own show, literally and figuratively. She was not only the star dancer, she was the dance maker and the business-savvy entrepreneur. As such, she served as precursor to a whole generation of dancers—mostly young

> women from America—whose fresh ideas and attitudes would prove to be as revolutionary a force in the theater as the incursion of African-American dance forms had already become in the ballroom .... [For modern dance] was not just about how to move; it was also about how art should be made and by whom. (Ibid)

In 1903, Angela Isadora Duncan of California declared a new era of dance as she traveled to Europe and took inspiration from Greek dance to develop a style unregulated by the social artifice—childlike, spontaneous, and expressive of "human spirit." Ruth St. Denis would follow in inventing new vocabularies that responded to the century's expressionist aesthetic, and so would male innovators such as Rudolf Laban, Maude Allen, and Ted Shawn. Most of these early modern movers attempted to bring the realms of the spiritual and the material in their dances, particularly Duncan, St. Denis, Shawn, and Fuller. In the 1920s and '30s, a second generation of modern dancers and choreographers such as Mary Wigman (Laban's student), Doris Humphrey and Martha Graham (St. Denis's students) emerged (Foster 1986, 145-47). Each created their own individual style and vocabulary that were derived from the everyday and earth-bound movements: walks, leaps, skips, jumps, falls, contractions. They also tackled themes that ranged from personal to political influences, from choreographic intuition to human emotion, as well as black, Greek, and ancient/ethnic cultures. However, in their endeavor to be unconventional, modern dance pioneers themselves developed their own respective conventions and vocabularies. Thus, there would be a so-called Graham technique based on contraction-and-release. Black women Pearl Primus and Katherine Dunham are known for their African-influenced style, Deborah Hay for her "dance as a communion" process, and Twyla Tharp for her eclectic, pedestrian movement combinations.

Amid these stirrings in early twentieth century America, modern dance was first performed in the Philippines through the *bodabil* (vaudeville) stage in 1926 by the Denishawn dancers led by Ruth St. Denis and her husband, Ted Shawn. Their repertoire was a combination of Western and Asian-inspired dances, among them was Shawn's *The Cosmic Dance of Shiva* and St. Denis' *A Japanese Court Dancer.* Austrian Kathe Hauser came to the country in 1932 to start a modern dance school named *Ausdrukstanz,* which means "creative or interpretative dance." Her fellow Viennese dancer Trudl Dubsky soon followed in 1937. A prolific modern choreographer, Trudl trained a host of local dancers including Ricardo Reyes, Lucio Sandoval, Corazon Generoso-Iñigo, Adina Rigor Ferrer, Remedios Villanueva Piñon, Remedios de Oteyza, Rosalia Merino-Santos, Lydia Gaston, and Mercy Lauchengco Drilon, among others. In the 1930s, a certain Felly Franquelli, one of Madame Adameit's students, established herself as an independent or solo dance artist and toured her performances in Europe. Katrina Makarova, a Russian émigré, also taught ballet in Manila. One of Makarova's students was Anita Kane, who later established her own Anita Kane Ballet Company, later renamed Pamana Ballet, which toured the country with classical and Filipino-themed performances. Rosalia Merino-Santos of the Far Eastern University Experimental Dance Troupe likewise made incursions into modern dance.

However, it was only after Alice Reyes set up the Alice Reyes Modern Dance Company at the Cultural Center of the Philippines (CCP) in 1970 that modern dance gradually earned a legitimate place in Philippine theatrical dance scene. After taking her MA in Dance abroad, Alice Reyes, daughter of Bayanihan dancer Ricardo Reyes, established the company which held annual summer workshops and performances and tapped local choreographies by Reyes herself, among them were Rosalia Merino-

Santos, Eddie Elejar, Tony Fabella, Gener Caringal, Luis Layag, and Basilio Esteban Villaruz. As the CCP's resident dance company, it was renamed CCP Dance Company and later, under the artistic directorship of Reyes, as Ballet Philippines, having annual performance seasons, provincial and international tours. Five notable women—Alice Reyes, Edna Vida, Denisa Reyes, Cecile Sicangco, and Agnes Locsin—as its artistic directors and choreographers sustained the company until it reached its twentieth year in 1990. Some of the company's modern works are Alice Reyes's *Itim Asu, Amada, Tales of the Manuvu,* and *Carmina Burana;* Denisa Reyes's *For the Gods, Siete Dolores,* and *Asong Ulol;* Agnes Locsin's *Igorot, Bagobo,* and *Encantada;* and Edna Vida's *Ensalada* and *Vision of Fire*. Other groups outside the CCP—the UP Dance Company, Makiling Ballet of the Philippine High School for the Arts, Powerdance, Quezon City Ballet, and other lesser-known regional dance schools such as those of Carmen Locsin in Davao, Fe Villarica of Cebu, Jess de Paz in Leyte, and Odon Sabarre of Tacloban—have produced modern works as well. More explorations in the modern and contemporary idiom in other venues can be found in the works of Enrico Labayen's former Lab. Projekt (1990), and Jojo Lucila and Ida Beltran's Chameleon Dance Company (*CCP Encyclopedia* 1994, 54-55).

Contemporary "Independents"

We have glimpsed in the preceding sections the process through which the dance establishment eventually co-opted and legitimated an originally dissident dance movement, as can be seen in the inclusion of modern dance in dance company repertoires and ballet school curricula. The colonization of the modern dance idiom incited the movement to be independent of the power structures surrounding the company system. It is in this context that contemporary "independents" have sprung.

Christy Adair uses the term "independents" to refer to independent artists who produce and practice dance outside the mainstream dance companies, usually financially self-sustained or with minimal funding. Adair sees how the dance company is limited by dominant social structures and hierarchies that are deeply established in large institutions. The question now is not just about demolishing gender hierarchies, for simply having women at the top positions without tearing down the same dominant notions on dance and culture merely repeats the same inequities of the previous powers-that-be, only this time it is set by another group of power players.

> Female directors and choreographers in ballet and contemporary dance are likely to reinforce dominant practices as they are working within the mainstream. Although women's work in these dance forms is important because, simply by the act of directing and/or choreographing they are challenging male supremacy, this is not where subversive images/dance practice are likely to emerge. *The subversives are likely to be the "independents," the dance workers in small- to middle-scale companies, the choreographers/performers/ directors working with limited budgets.* (Adair 1992, 200; italics mine)

The very structures in which large dance and cultural institutions operate have to be themselves confronted. And this requires a certain critical distance that the independent dance practitioner gains as s/he dares to set-up outside the dominant system, carrying out her or his self-defined oppositional practices and politics.*

* During the Martial Law years, four companies existed outside the Marcos' mantle, notably Dance Theatre Philippines, Dance Concert Company, Hariraya Ballet, and Manila Metropolis Ballet, producing both classical and contemporary works.

In Europe and America, the phenomenon of independent dancing has become more prominent from the 1980s up to the present as more and more dancers seek more relevant and responsive frameworks to suit their new ways of dancing and dance-making. In the UK, for one, there exists an organized support system called the Independent Dance Artists' Network which offers assistance to independent professional dance artists throughout the country. As more and more dancers leave their original home companies, searching for more decentralized ways of training, creating and practicing dance, they have set up shop in the idiom of independence and dignity and define a dance aesthetic of their own.

In the Philippines, those who trained in the local dance schools and companies have also gone to practice abroad and founded their own independent dance idiom, notably Fil-Am dancer Kristin Jackson with her Kristin Jackson Dance in 1988. This has also been the case of The Lab. Projekt by Enrico Labayen, a former Ballet Philippines (BP) dancer who went on to experiment with his own movement style and philosophy. From 1990 to 1994 Labayen mainly worked with Myra Beltran, also formerly of Dance Concert Company and BP, holding daily dance classes in the Beltran studio and performing in various non-proscenium venues such as the Baguio Arts Festival. When Labayen left in 1994 for San Francisco, California to found his own independent group called Labayen/SF, Myra was inspired to pursue independent practice in her own terms. This was realized when Myra formally set up Dance Forum in 1997 and opened the Beltran Studio-theater as her own independent performance space. In 2000, after a full fourteen-year stint as chief choreographer and artistic director of Ballet Philippines, Agnes Locsin decided to return to her Davao roots, to teach and create dances in her mother's 57-year-old dance school, this time as an independent dance artist.

Currently, a younger generation of dancers trained in Ballet Philippines have also left the traditional dance company system, notably Christine Maranan, Paul Morales, and Dwight Rodrigazo. Finding their own independent and eclectic idiom in dance, they established Airdance, a dance school-cum-group that accepts choreography work for commercial projects. Theater-trained Jose Jay Cruz of PETA also has his Dancing Wounded Contemporary Dance Commune which now closely collaborates with Myra Beltran's Dance Forum.

In more recent times, the term "independent" has especially gained more footing in Philippine dance. In 2005, the first Contemporary Dance Map was held in celebration of International Dance Day with the support of the National Commission for Culture and the Arts. This was pioneered by independent dance practitioners, notably chaired by Myra Beltran in collaboration with members of the World Dance Alliance-Philippines. Tapping various small independently-run performing groups in Quezon City such as Airdance, Green Papaya Art Projects, UP Dance Company, Quezon City Ballet, and Chameleon Dance Company, the project literally mapped-out the alternative terrain of contemporary dancing via their performances in their own small, private studios, definitely away from the Manila-centered and established performance spaces such as the CCP theatres. This was followed by the first Contemporary Dance Festival in 2006 entitled *Wi-Fi Body,* held this time at the CCP theatres and also pioneered by the same dance groups but now with more organizational backing and funding, as if claiming the established center stage where only major dance companies were known to perform.

It is amidst this continuing emergence of a new independent aesthetics in dance that I have chosen to foreground three particular women—Myra Beltran, Kristin Jackson, and Agnes Locsin—who have articulated their aesthetics and narratives as independent dance-makers even before the term "independent dance" became a popular buzzword in Philippine dance, as they have visibly challenged certain set ideas on the culture of dance and developed with their self-defined mold of dancing independently.

CHAPTER 4

Movements from the Margins: When Women Dance Independently

Seen through my lenses as a dance researcher, I now explore the stories of each independent dance-maker. Each narrative in this chapter is woven across my personal encounters with them and the critical perspectives stirred in those meetings.

Each of these narratives begins with a personal note that describes my previous knowledge of them, which then unfolds into a more substantive narrative about each dance artist as I came to know them in the research and writing process. The logic of this re-telling revolves around the critical moments when they shifted from traditional to independent dance practice. As historical narratives, these stories highlight their formative years as women dancers and dance-makers and the turning points in their careers from institutional to independent dance practice, as well as the present challenges and prospects in their chosen aesthetic of independently producing and creating dances.

My longest standing encounter is with Myra Beltran, who also happens to be the most articulate in defining herself as an independent woman dancer in contemporary Philippine dance, and whose dances and aesthetics I have extensively written and researched about in most of my graduate papers. The next encounter is with Kristin Jackson, a New York-based Fil-Am independent dancer who I fortunately got to meet in the course of my research process while she was serving her stint at the University of the Philippines as a visiting lecturer of the College of Music dance program in 2003. And finally, former Ballet Philippines chief choreographer and artistic director Agnes Locsin, whose celebrated work *Igorot* I have written about in one graduate research paper. My initial interest in Agnes' choreography was further sparked when I learned of her major shift from being a main player in a major cultural institution to a dance teacher in her mother's studio in Davao City.

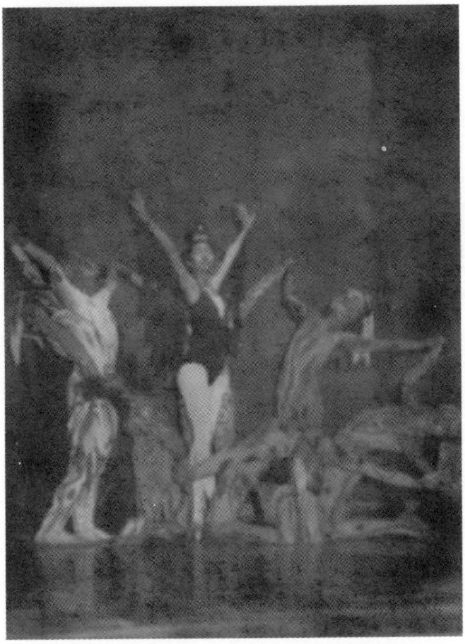

From the ballet *Mir-i-nisa* where Myra was the Black Pearl during the underwater scene, 1977.

So I lay down here the threads of three stories, individual yet intertwined, as we would witness them in this re-telling.

Myra Beltran: Dancing and other Necessities

A frail-looking woman in white chemise begins to undulate on the floor, as if her legs were bound and her arms clipped within that small space. Struggle is written on her face, emphasizing the gesture of being held captive by an unseen force. As Ravel's music ends, the woman quietly rises to her feet, her back towards the audience, unfolding her arms and opening her chest upwards as if to bask in the wings of newfound freedom.

Watching this austere and minimalist dance piece at the UP Theater was, to me, a meaningful eye-opener that dance could be rendered in another way. As an avid dance audience member then taking respite from ballet practice, I was myself only used to performing and watching pleasant-looking classical ballets. This first encounter with contemporary dance was personally significant as a young dancer in that it spurred me to question the traditional values and valuational criteria surrounding the idea of what should be considered a "beautiful dance" as was taught to me early on, mainly in the ballet school.

The dancer was Myra Beltran in her self-choreographed piece entitled *Becoming*, a solo from a larger dance called *Birdwoman*. It was 1995, and the Philippines played host to the Contemporary Dance Festival at the state university theater.

Years later I would find myself watching several of Myra's other works, this time in her own studio-theater which she shares with her sister's and brother-in-law's Chameleon Dance Company, unassumingly situated within the Beltrans' residential compound at 38 West Avenue in Quezon City.

It was while watching Myra's non-conventional works that I grew to be interested in researching about the ways of a self-defined independent dancer, and how a woman mainly trained in ballet convention could possibly articulate herself in an alternative, nearly nebulous, idiom in the Philippine dance world.

Becoming of a dancer

Myra Victoria Beltran traces her foundational training in dance to the age of 12, when she took her first ballet lessons with Vella Damian that her godmother paid for. She remembers repeating the same steps from her first ballet class for one whole week until her next class, progressing in her ballet technique from then on.

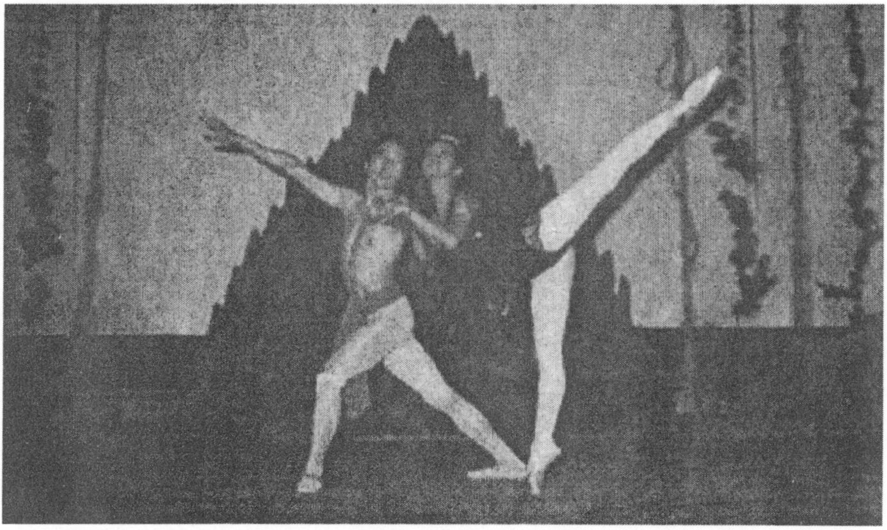

From the ballet *Mir-i-nisa* where Myra was the Black Pearl during the underwater scene, 1977.

Myra was a product of the efforts to form a national dance company under the Ballet Federation of the Philippines, which rehearsed in the Beltrans' studio space from 1978 to the early 1980s. The studio was originally built by her uncles in the 1960s to host their judo club activities, and was later turned into a dance studio when Vella Damian rented it to hold ballet classes.

Myra, born in 17 November 1960, was the fifth child of six siblings. When she started taking ballet classes with Vella Damian, all her other sisters followed suit. Eventually, it was only she and her younger sister, Ida Beltran (now Lucila), who pursued dancing as a career.

From early on, however, Myra felt uninterested in the idea of mere virtuosity in dance technique; she felt that there had to be more to dancing than just looking "pretty and good" in front of a ballet master. In 1978, with Martial Law still hovering, she was enrolled in the speech and drama program in UP. However, she thought that there was no way that she could make it as a dancer in a country amidst troubled political conditions. A year later, at age 19, she left the country for the US thinking of pursuing a dance degree, but later decided to fly to Germany to look for what she could not yet define. From 1981 to 1982, Myra danced with the Ballet of Oldenburg in Germany. In 1982, she moved to Yugoslavia and danced with the Ballet of the Theater Prishtina until 1986. In dancing professionally abroad, she experienced a sense of displacement from her own culture, and the concomitant racial prejudice of being "brown" in a European country. She recalls the experience of being a dancer in a foreign land:

> Dancing in Germany was really sad. When I was here in the country as a young dancer, I was taught to excel. But when you're abroad, you realize you have brown skin. All of the prejudice that overseas workers go through I went through. I realize that

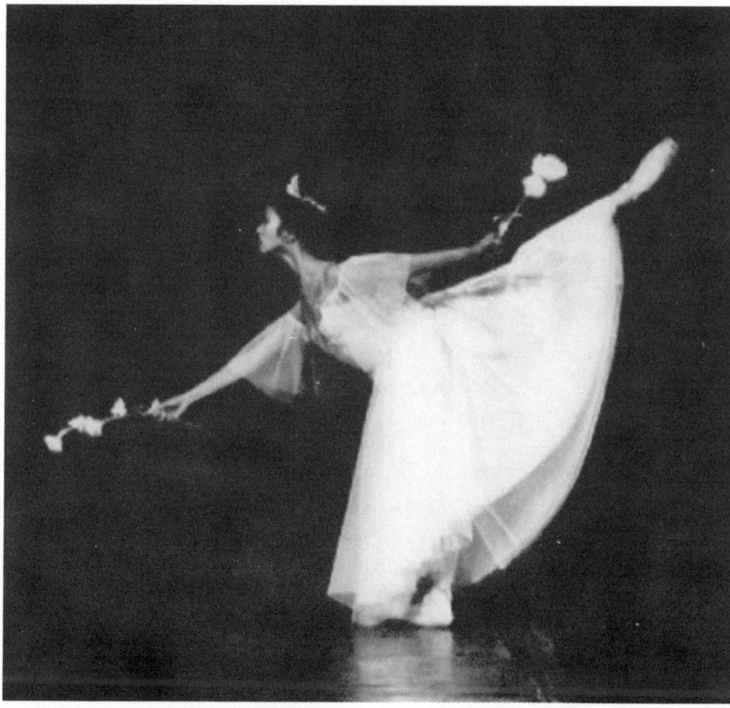

Myra as Myrtha in the ballet *Giselle*, 1982.

dancing is pure but not if you're brown-skinned with a Filipino passport. They won't give you a work permit and it's hard to get into their theater system. I always asked myself when I was abroad, "when will I be strong enough to come home?" I knew what was there [in Germany] and didn't want it. It's still not your culture. It's interesting for a while *pero kakatukin ka pa rin ng kultura mo*. I think I left home too early and too young – at age 19. By age 20 I had my own flat with a salary of my own. But I left home young because there's a part of me that had to be resolved. I questioned everything. At that time also, everybody was questioning the political situation in Europe. At that time students in Germany would go out in the streets to openly question.[1]

This indelible experience caused her to further interrogate dance and realize its necessary cultural grounded-ness. Thus, amidst her physical and cultural dislocation, she made dancing her own mode of self-empowerment:

> Dancing to me was something real that I hung on to. Other things seemed so superficial. Art was real. But then there was not much concept of country and culture. You're ashamed—*ang alam mo lang may* martial law. But I had not much fervor, and I guess some dancers are like that. *Parang* they're country-less and they profess to art that's like that. But I don't think it's possible.
>
> When I was overseas the only thing that really saved me was my dancing. Not just financially but physically. Dancing is my meditation, my empowerment. When things were going bad, I was so confused, I'd just dance and it would set me thinking right. I came home in 1986, still questioning dance and everything else but I was still at it, dancing. How can you let go of something that in a way saved you? That's why I still hang on to the art up to this day.

Myra finally came home in 1986 for personal reasons: her brother had died and she was still nursing wounds from her own broken marriage in Yugoslavia. These potent experiences all added up to provoke more personal questions, not just about her dancing, but about herself and the direction she was to take from there. The country was still in revelry after the EDSA phenomenon, as people found more democratic openings and spaces in nearly all aspects of society. For artists, this also meant more room for expression and growth.

Within this generally hopeful atmosphere, Myra decided to keep doing what she had always wanted to do—dance. She joined CCP's Ballet Philippines (BP) from 1987 to 1991. In between, she took a Bachelor of Arts degree in Business Economics in UP, mainly to fulfill her parents' desire for her to do something for a living besides dance, which did not earn much to begin with. Her undergraduate course in business proved to be useful years later when she decided to become an independent dancer which involved fundraising and marketing, aside from the usual choreography work, directing and performing.

Myra's predisposition to go independent began in 1991 after leaving BP and being invited by former BP dancer Enrico Labayen to join his experimental group The Lab. Projekt with a few other dancers. Myra's initial headways in exploring her own dance idiom at the family studio since 1989 drew Enrico to tap and invite her into his own independent explorations. Eventually, only the two of them were left holding daily classes and movement studies in the Beltran studio. In the late 1980s, Myra also actively participated and performed for her visual artists-friends in the Baguio Arts Festival, improvising dances for the installation works of Bencab, Pepito Bosch, Kidlat Tahimik and Roberto Villanueva. It was in these spaces that she first learned to dance in non-proscenium spaces and found affinity to art as ritual. She also felt strongly for the vision of other artists to decentralize art and bring it back to the communities—a far cry from her BP and overseas dance experience, which she felt was not responsive to social realities. Her dancing in several Baguio Art Fests gave cultural grounding to her attempts at choreography and defining her own "choreographic vision."

When Enrico left the country in 1994, Myra declared herself an independent dancer. Two young dancers who were her's and Enrico's students at the Philippine High School for the Arts would join them occasionally with the Lab. Projekt classes but eventually went to other established dance companies. Up till now, Myra maintains this link with younger dance students whom she'd invite to cast in her subsequent shows, especially after Dance Forum's launch and her private studio's opening as a theater-performance space in 1997.

Moreover, Myra's exposure to other local women artists who were part of the 1995 Beijing Conference on Women—namely poet Merlinda Bobis, dancer and researcher Ligaya Amilbangsa, singer Grace Nono, among others—significantly inspired her to think about what it means to be a woman artist. At that time, she declared herself a "solo woman dance artist," something she felt that nobody else had dared to assert within her milieu. Myra thus assertively claims that she was the first to call herself an independent dancer in the country. In watching her dances, as well as in our subsequent interviews and conversations, she is consistent and conscious in calling her aesthetic "independent," defining it as being self-produced and self-defined outside the major cultural institutions. Her exposure to independent dance groups during her stay in Europe has also made her more informed about how she would define that yet unknown path in Philippine contemporary dance she had wanted to make a mark in.

Aesthetics of her own

Although different in style and aesthetics from Labayen, Myra initially took inspiration from his alternative, almost underground image in dance. Myra would also employ his multi-gravitational technique—which makes use of hanging ropes and cloths for dancers to explore movements with—in some of her future works. Despite Labayen's strong influence in Myra's initial independent explorations, Myra found her own vocabulary in dance that eventually set her apart from the former.

> The work I like is one of warmth. Of not cold manipulation of forms but an exploration of form, perhaps a manipulation but

> with a total idea or feeling in mind, not for its sake alone—of real sharing of experience. *I believe though that this is done still very much in dialogue with one's dance tradition. I think one should be conscious of where in the history of dance one is taking it, no vague assumptions about aesthetics, but deliberate choices.* (Email correspondence, May 2, 2004; italics mine)

We now find Myra's own version of contemporary dance aesthetic as mainly a re-functioning of conventional ballet steps, grounding them in her body and personal realities as a specific type of woman. This is a deliberate choice on her part, claiming herself "a feminist but not of the virago kind." Her idea of moving around in small imaginary spaces with delicate, sometimes angular steps, is opposed to the ballet aesthetic of delivering grand steps that open widely into the large proscenium stage. Myra is also into exploring movements using a lot of floor work based on the idea of the body being gravity-bound, as opposed to the flight and elevation in classical ballet dancing. Even with the use of ropes and cloths which she would sometimes hang on to in exploring movements, it is the idea of heaviness and anguish as the pervading mood and emotion—never of the ballerina's pleasing lightness—that is strongly highlighted in her facial demeanor.

One of Myra's philosophies is that of having a dialogue with one's dance tradition and history, thereby making dance a mode of sharing experience; this she likens to a ritual since it is communal and collective. We see this philosophy embodied in her productions that show the collaborative nature of art and dance-making, and illuminate the possibility of dialogue with various artists and the traditions from where they come from. Noteworthy among them is *Daughters of Necessity: Women Solos in Dance* (2000),[2] significantly timed in March for women's month. The title *Daughters of Necessity* alluded to the Greek goddess and mother of invention Necesitas. Myra felt that the metaphoric character aptly captured how women's necessity to create and reinvent their selves is best done by acknowledging the choreographic works of their foremothers, as well as their current work as contemporary women dancers.

Daughters highlights the multiplicity of women's creative expression and the genealogical thread weaving them amidst their differentiated and diverse sources of thematic inspiration and modes of expressing creativity. In this project, she reconstructed the solo works of three Filipina female choreographers—Alice Reyes' *Dandansoy*, Corazon Inigo's *Sisa,* and Denisa Reyes' *One-Ton Pinay*—with whom she finds affinity in Philippine modern dance history. Myra invited two other former BP dancers, Joanne Ko de la Calzada and Christine Maranan to perform the reconstructed solos.[3] Joanne rendered *Dandansoy,* a modern dance inspired by festive and graceful folk dance movements, which was part of BP's earlier Filipiniana repertoire. Christine rendered *Sisa,* a dance portrayal of a tragic character from Rizaliana which entailed acting out in anguished movements the story of a mother as madwoman. *One-Ton Pinay,* the most contemporary and eclectic of the three, was executed by Myra. Here, she played a modern-day Filipina and US émigré, expressing in various frenzied movements her being caught up in the many layers of dance cultures and traditions that have colonized her body politic. Meanwhile, the three women also presented their very own solo choreographies. Joanne performed her religious-themed *Introspection: Cycle 3*, where she recited and interpreted the words from spiritual activist Kiara Lubich's poetry. Christine danced her journey from childhood to young womanhood in *Tender Journeys*. Lastly, Myra's *Unbearable Lightness,* a direct allusion to Milan Kundera's book, shows the duality of heaviness and lightness expressed through the use of floor work, of lying and kneeling with one foot pointed and the other flexed. In this existential, angst-ridden piece, Myra once again exemplifies her characteristic idea of "woundedness" and the evocation of heaviness. Finally, the show culminated with Myra's *Daughters of Necessity,* danced by the three women in short white chemise and plain white ballet shoes. In this recapitulation, they echoed each other's movements of circling, carrying, embracing, and walking forward to an imagined psychic space expressed by their far-reaching gaze, as if projecting a promising future for them and other women in their midst.

Besides the three dancers, women visual artists were also given space to exhibit their works along the entrance path leading to the studio-theater. Among them were Lorna Israel, Sandra Torrijos, Maita Beltran, Christina Ramilo, Teena Saulo, Irma Lacorte, and Bing Concepcion. Lighting was by Shari Villa.

Necessary advocacy

Notably, one of the shows of *Daughters* was sponsored by Woman-Health Philippines, an advocacy group for women's reproductive rights. Held at UP's Wilfrido Ma. Guerrero Theater, among the audience were WomanHealth's women partners from urban poor communities—particularly Pasig and Novaliches—whom they had organized in promoting health education and in advancing their rights in policy advocacy and community organizing.

Mercy Fabros, WomanHealth advocacy and campaign coordinator, shares the group's rationale for tapping the production of *Daughters*: "*Mahalaga sa amin ang pagmamahal sa katawan, dahil 'yan ang* medium of expression, to claim and self-empower. *Mahalaga sa amin ang sayaw, mga ritwal,* exercises *upang mapanindigan at malikha ang sarili,* to recreate yourself continuously. *Di ka makakasayaw kung di ka umaalpas.* You have to totally give yourself when you dance, *may pag-angkin ka sa sarili.*"

Myra speaks of this collaboration with a women's NGO as "an organic process," recounting that it was after Mercy saw her *Star Maiden* (1997) that she was tapped to convey, in dance form, the group's research findings about "Negotiating Reproductive Rights." Myra relates, "Mercy saw that somehow, in my dances I had captured what their research was trying to convey. I performed for them, as their research was presented in an innovative way, in drama form, because the method of gathering data was through storytelling. I was the presentation's synthesis, after the open forum. Princess Nemenzo [also of WomanHealth] and she have always come to my performances since then."

Daughters' mode of empowering and sharing dance with fellow women artists can be found in a much earlier work entitled *Fragile Circle* (1998), where she invited visual artists Lia Tayag, Karen Flores, Katti Sta. Ana, and Alma Quinto to present their works as part of the dance. Shakira Villa provided the show's lighting design. In *Fragile Circle,* Myra wanted to highlight the "fragile circle," formed among women artists, which she set to movement while reciting selected poems from Jane Hirshfield's collection entitled *Women in Praise of the Sacred.* She was joined by younger dancers Catherine Urmenita and Donna Miranda. The three dancers performed slow and small gestures while seated in three-tiered risers, as if emphasizing that delicate and small "feminine" space women have been socially conditioned to move in.

It is in these two specific dance collaborative productions[4] that Myra has subtly threaded the multiple connections between the art world and prevailing social realities, especially those concerning women—her fellow sisters taking differentiated paths within a diverse women's movement.

All these years, Myra has also cultivated a distinct audience mostly composed of UP students and faculty, theater people, and NGO workers.

Space-claiming as empowerment

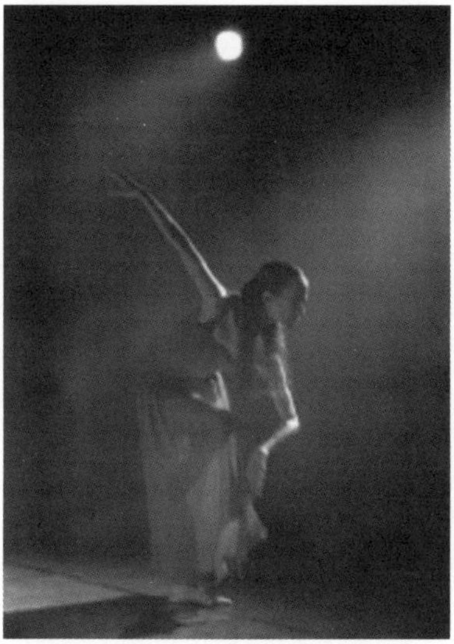

Myra dancing "Damas Confuria" choreographed by Enrico Labayen in 2003.

In claiming the intimately small studio-theater as a regular venue for both her classes and performance works, Myra has made a marked difference in her very practice of dance. Her non-proscenium space with three sides opening to wild backyard greenery makes her dance space homey, almost provincial, and easily refreshing for dancers tired from hours of dance practice—much unlike the air-conditioned buildings that house ballet studios, which further add artificiality and formality to dance as an activity far removed and alienated from everyday life. The seats surrounding the center stage resemble casual basketball bleachers which do not privilege any one particular viewing position; each viewer seated from any point can partake of the dance, making the show more accessible and democratic. This smallness and accessibility provided by the space also erases the demarcation between art and life, between performers and viewers, which is one of the pervasive illusions created in grand proscenium theaters.[5]

Indeed, behind this space is the deliberate choice to be an independent woman dancer, with a clear sense of agenda and vision of what it means to be non-traditional in creating and practicing dance.

> The reason I went independent in the first place was because I felt there was another process to dance-making that had the

> creative process foremost in mind. I like sharing, collaborating, bringing forth your own ideas and feelings about issues or events of the day, or opinion on history, a performance, etc. and I felt that could happen in the creative process. I feel that an authentic work of art is a result of the energies of people working with you, I don't believe of a choreographer as "an all-knowing, all-seeing person" like a god that usually traditionally-trained dancers tend to think or imbue those qualities to their directors. So I guess that whole process shows in the work. (Email correspondence, May 2, 2004)

Apart from Myra's collaborative productions, her practice of teaching dance also embodies this politics. Katherine Sanchez—one of Myra's long-time dancers in the Lab. Projekt and also a former student at Makiling High School—relates how she felt "not judged" while dancing in Myra's space, in contrast to the feeling of being "just an employee" of ballet masters in traditional dance companies where there is a more rigid structure and strictness in following ballet technique. Myra's class still follows the rudiments of ballet classes—barre work and center work—but with freer, more personalized and improvised movements that use basic ballet steps to get in touch with the body, not so much to show off one's form. Myra calls this the "science" of ballet, which she says has made the dance "deeper" for her in understanding her own bodily gestures and expressions, and what they personally mean to her. She claims that she has not let go of ballet completely but simply made it work for her, instead of allowing it to erase her own personal expression.

Observing Myra's classes with younger female ballet dancers, and having joined two classes several years back, I noticed her distinct use of pliés, which are graceful knee-bends in ballet, but which she executes with an edgy push on the floor. In her pliés, there is a marked push as the legs bend, and the back is semi-arched, opposed to the ideal of straight lines in classical ballet dancing. This utilization of edgy plies—combined with all other steps, from *tendus, glissés, pas de cheval, retirés,* among others—is the basic backbone throughout her class, giving her movements a contemporary texture. In her classes, she would share to her dancers her ideas about being sensitive to their bodies' "interaction with gravity," the idea of "forces in opposition," the "flow of physics," of experiencing "the spiral in the square," the "whole circle of movement." Her center work is also composed of the usual ballet adagio and allegro combinations, where ballet steps of *tombé, pas de bourée,* and *pirouette* are combined with modernized straight upward arms. She cautions dancers to do it not with the usual classical grace but with emphasis on the forcefulness of the "slide, flick and glide." This, she says, is how she has made ballet contemporary, that is, more responsive to her in getting to know her body as a woman.

Myra's reappropriation of ballet is also exemplified in her infrequent use of the pointe shoes, the classical ballerina's trademark footwear, which helps in creating an illusion of lightness. This hardened pair of satin shoes usually causes the dancer considerable pain—bunions, corns, calluses, and bleeding toes—which she hides by executing the technically demanding steps with pleasing grace. In keeping with her contemporary idiom, Myra rarely dances on pointes nowadays; when she does, it is to express edginess, grounded-ness and an anguished angularity in her performances, not the ideal litheness of the sylph-like romanticized ballerina. She says that when she uses pointes in class, it is simply a way to "get to know my own body." And for Myra, this body is that of a contemporary Filipina dancing woman, working beyond the traditional classicism embedded in the ballet idiom that was her and many other female dancers' initial training.

In terms of creating relationships of camaraderie and professionalism with her dancers, she has this to share:

> I value my dancers, their opinions and feelings. I talk to them a lot to create camaraderie. They also get professional fees with transportation allowance, and they are served food in rehearsals. Everybody in the crew has a good time and the feeling of belonging is created. *And I tell my dancers to be a person dancing, not just a dancer.*[6] (Italics mine)

Having gone through the harsh working conditions in Germany and in traditional ballet companies, Myra intends to treat her fellow artists the way she thinks dance artists should be treated, that is, with value and respect, both in economic and emotional terms.

On the side, to keep up with the financial requirements of Dance Forum, Myra would take a few people who would occasionally express interest to take her classes, though she refuses to make her dance classes commercial like in formal ballet schools. In the summer of 2004, she was invited to teach dancers in Taiwan and was also part of the faculty in contemporary dance at the CCP Summer Dance Workshop. Occasionally, she would also teach movement class at the Asian Institute of Liturgy and Music, take choreographic projects for plays, and at times be a testing officer at TESDA (Technical Education and Skills Development Authority).

Acknowledging traditions and histories

Myra's other more recent works are similarly woven around her history and identity as a contemporary Filipina woman dancer. *Confuria* (2003), a trio set to the music of Bella Bartok, originated from the idea of the Latin American samba, a form of prayer practiced in colonial Latin

America. Appropriating "samba," which connotes a similar meaning of worship in Filipino language, Myra made the dance into a contemporary ritual of celebrating female fertility. *Confuria* is built around sharp and jagged moves. This, together with the dancers' use of black miniskirt and translucent blouse and their occasional derisive faces in gazing at each other and their audience, evoke women's sensuality and religious subversion.

Although mostly a tribute, another significant work that was meant to be a ritual of story-telling was a restaging of *Damas,* a choreographic work by her most influential mentor Enrico Labayen.[7] Simply entitled *Episodes in 3 Parts,* Myra recreated the piece in her recent May 2004 show at the CCP experimental theater. Using multimedia video footage of Enrico's solo and duet parts with her, Myra improvised the original dance with her own movements. The work tackles their intimacy and professional relationship as fellow dancers, and the often painful idea of being set apart by time and circumstance.

In the third episode of the original dance, Enrico recited vignettes of several AIDS victims' names and their experiences, finally ending with an acknowledgement that he himself is a victim of the yet incurable disease. In Myra's re-creation, she simply showed slow-motioned video images of Enrico's heart-rending confessional piece, but his voice was muted by the background jazz song "I'll be seeing you." Simultaneously, Myra danced and recited lines from various authors, including her own, which spoke of her personal dialogue and experience of Enrico and the dance tradition they have shared: *Art is long and life is short, and success is very far off / Do we not live life based on selected fictions? / Are there shortcuts in the sky, summer moon? / I still have my memory, I still have my song.*

Myra ends the piece using hanging ropes and cloths, the characteristic style her mentor is known for. As she twisted her arms around a white cloth, using it to turn her around in spirals, the opposing forces of gravity and flight work with her body. Her posture as she reached the point of stillness can be read as her surrender to the forces of fate.

Story-sharing as ritual

Apart from the aforementioned works, Myra's cultural groundedness is also inscribed in her love of telling stories through dance. This is most clearly seen in *Star Maiden* (1997), her first full production, which marked the opening of her studio as her own performance space. *Star Maiden* is a recreation of a local folklore about the origination of the Filipino people from the love shared between a star maiden and a farmer. For her, this production set the tone of what was to be the aesthetics of her future works as an independent dance artist.

Star Maiden was initially an offshoot of *Birdwoman* (1995)—an earlier work based on a Japanese tale—which Myra performed in Casa San Miguel in Zambales, her musician-friend Alfonso Bolipata's artistic space. Wanting to find local connections with the Japanese legend of the Bird Woman, Myra researched for a similar tale in our culture. She found two versions of the same story from Cordillera and Bukidnon, both resonating the themes of love, betrayal, and the birth of a people.

In her evening-long rendition of the tale, played in the background before each dance was her voice telling the star maiden's story in prose-poetic form which she herself composed. The performance began with a narration of how three star maidens once descended the earth to bathe in a river and a farmer who saw them hid one of the star maiden's wings so that he could ask her to be his wife. It was from this marriage of the farmer (earth) and the star maiden (heaven) that the Filipino people came to be. Myra adds a twist to the story, however, by exploring how one day, after years of living as a mortal on earth, the star maiden found one of her wings earlier hidden by the farmer. It was from this point in the story that Myra's series of seven solo dances began.

In a journal entry she shared with the author,[8] Myra mirrors her close personal affinity with the star maiden's tale: as a Philippine legend that echoes her cultural roots; and as a female-centered narrative which resonates deeply with her own experience as a contemporary Filipina woman dancing.

> The solo work chronicles the awakening of the Star Maiden. Essentially, there was a betrayal there by the farmer, because he had stolen her wings. I wanted my wings back! But I also had to ask myself the deep meaning of this story and if I wanted my wings back, to be free again, so to speak, to fly and explore, I had to find this relationship to the farmer, and I wanted this to be positive and complete. I wanted this story to live in that present time. The solos track the landscape of Zambales, which I sense bodily when I am at the Casa San Miguel—an abandoned attic (Silver Streak of Wings), under the full moon (Beginning), by a river or stream (Cloak of Midnight), up a mountain (Rock Me to Sleep), the ocean and the impossibility of crossing it (Air), being up in the clouds (Song) and just back to me (Star Maiden).
>
> But, and this is important, each solo is a metaphor for the human condition, like a legend on its own, so that as the journey is made through a geographic space that evokes the Philippines, it is also an inner journey.
>
> I wanted each solo to connote different legends in Philippine myth, at the same time, being re-told by the body of one woman. This is important, and makes the work multi-layered and not

> entirely, "personal." This is what gives it its ethnicity, the music connotes the "silvery strings" of the stars, and some of it is quite "popular" and accessible classical music, and this is by design. Multi-layeredness is better intuited by this accessibility (Myra's diary entry, December 25, 2003).

Myra began to explore her own personalized contemporary movement idiom in her *Star Maiden* solos, each of which told simple stories of inner struggle and self-confrontation. In *Rock Me to Sleep*, she painstakingly pushed a rock on an imagined mountain, until she reached the other side of the stage and finally rested in sleep atop the rock. In *Air*, she stood on two elevated pieces of stone-like islands, which she used to laboriously navigate across an imaginary geography that stretched up to the other side of the stage, until eventually she reached a bigger island, standing on it with a look of relief on her face. The next dance is *Song*, where—with one arm free and the other supporting her floor-bound movements amidst a circle of white rose petals on stage—she articulated the movement of the star maiden being brought upwards back to the heavens by clouds. In the final act, *Star Maiden*, she victoriously danced and glided across rose petals, still with that angular edginess and melancholy emotiveness of having taken a mortal and earthly body, but with a sense of freedom for having finally retuned home to the heavens.

Myra relates how her first dance production has defined the style and trajectory of her future works from thereon:

> I love this work, though it might not be a "complete" work of art. It is the seed by which all my subsequent explorations follow. The exploration of space is an inner space, which means that the physical space covered by the one body is not that great in the normally accepted dance sense, and that in itself is a political choice. In the Philippines, there are not enough venues for dance,

> and in the provinces, hardly. To create out of limitation, and thus, also to finally say that "space is an encounter between moment and relationship" and not "physical" space, but space in the mind's eye – this was the challenge of Star Maiden, and that's why I love this work. It opened up new possibilities for seeing things that were already present in Birdwoman. That exploration took me far to other bodies and other works. It was decidedly a new aesthetic and with the opening of the studio space as a performance space, a breakthrough. I love that courageous woman, forging it, braving the wind in her face, with a lot of faith (Ibid).

In 2005 and 2006, Myra pioneered a series of collaborative performances with other emerging local independent dance artists which was innovatively called "Contemporary Dance Map," suggesting the unusual itinerary of showing dances within small alternative dance venues in Quezon City. As chairperson of the Choreographer's Network of the World Dance Alliance Philippines, Myra facilitated the presentation of independent choreographies in six small and alternative dance venues within the locality which proved to be a refreshing substitute to the large-scale Manila-centered performances that usually happen at the CCP. The dance groups and venues tapped were Dance Forum, Airdance, UP Dance Company, Green Papaya Art Projects, Chameleon Dance Theater, Dancing Wounded, and Quezon City Ballet. This was followed by the first independent contemporary dance festival in the country called "WiFi Body" held at various venues of the CCP in August 2006.

With these new steps at collaboration with a new and young generation of independent dance artists, Myra says that she is not envious of the "confusion" that she notices in today's emerging independent artists, and remains proud of the grounding she has developed within her dancing life.

> Perhaps, it would have been easy to go on the far end of the "conceptual" route that current contemporary dance sometimes veers to, following the Western avant-garde. But I had the fortune to be offered grounding, to have always asked myself how I would connect to ordinary women, both contemporary and maybe pre-colonial, this was my grounding. By this, I was able to relate my practice to—maybe it is trite to say it—to land, to environment, and therefore, to story. These stories from which Star Maiden arose, from beginnings, allowed me to choose simplicity over complexity, while still being many-layered. It gave me the "economy" that has also given me resilience, and a practice which is able to accomodate the many changes I experience as a woman, both bodily and emotionally. I do not mind being "representational" nor does it also prevent me from shifting positions when I choose to. All of this gave me a grounding for which my practice can be seen in a shifting continuum but in an integrated sense. I do not envy the confusion of the current generation, and I wish that they could peel the layers that would then expose their true grounding. (E-mail correspondence, October 24, 2006)

It is with this boldness to persist in transgressing boundaries—grounded in a storied past yet conscious of her present place and time—that Myra lives up to her clear vision of herself and her self-defined path in contemporary independent dance in the country.

Kristin Jackson:
Beyond the Disquietude of Diaspora

My first meeting with Kristin Jackson was in a café in UP, after having been initially introduced to her only through text messaging. She was staying in the university for a few more months to fulfill her Fulbright grant to teach in the College of Music dance program. While she was busy teaching and creating dances for students, we exchanged stories through interviews and conversations and I got to watch her works performed at the CCP and the UP Abelardo Hall. She had invited me to her place, a condominium unit bare and neatly arranged, a few days before leaving the country. We watched a student recital called *Higanti* thereafter at the Abelardo Hall and shared each other's critiques of the dance that supposedly deconstructed the classic *Giselle* ballet. More conversations followed through e-mail after she had left for New York. In sharing these stories, Kristin had been gentle, quiet, clear and open; her insights gradually shed more light into my research over time, in talks and correspondences, made of personal musings and clear recollections of what it meant to dance in her own time, and what it still means now that her dancing has found a home in a place other than where she was born and grew up in.

Formative years

The formative years of Kristin Jackson's artistic practice began in 1957, as a five-year-old girl who walked from her house in Taft Avenue, Manila to Anita Kane's neighboring ballet school to watch ballet classes. She remembers "falling in love" with the dance she had seen, so that for several weeks, she would repeat at home the steps she saw from the class. Upon seeing this, her parents decided to enroll her in Kane's dance studio.

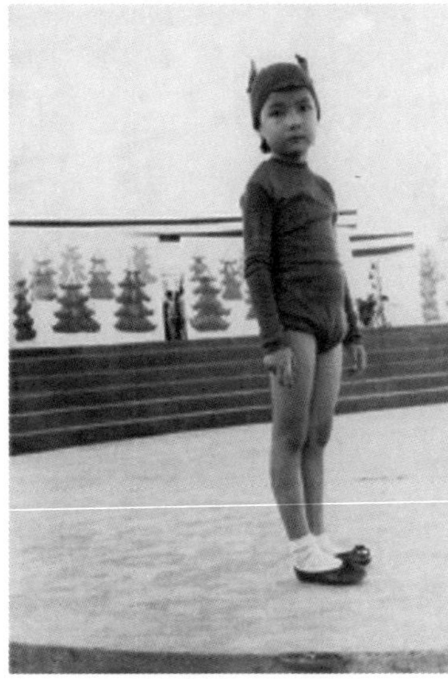

Kristin Jackson as a "mouse" in Anita Kane's Philippine production of *The Nutcracker* (1957).

Later, she felt with much disappointment that she was not meant to make a career of ballet, after not being cast to dance in one of Ms. Kane's annual recitals—what with the absences from ballet classes she incurred during her vacation with her parents in the US. She realized how consistent practice and constant self-discipline were very much necessary in order to be a good dancer.

Her mother, a nurse and native of Mauban, Quezon, and her father, an Irish-American employed at Clark Air Base in Pampanga, thought that she should stop dancing upon seeing her early disenchantment with dance. But it was her father's advice for her to simply "take things in stride" that quelled the frustration in the young dancing Kristin. This same advice became a guiding principle she would take on for life, especially in her choice of dance as a lifetime profession. Kristin reckons that it was the first and important test of her commitment to dance.

Thus, Kristin continued on with her dance classes, learning much from Kane's pedagogy of "valuing quality of movement over pure technique" and for instilling in her a commitment to the art of dance. Ms. Kane would cast her in a challenging solo in *Les Sylphides* at the young age of fourteen. In the late 1960s when Anita Kane returned to the US, Kristin

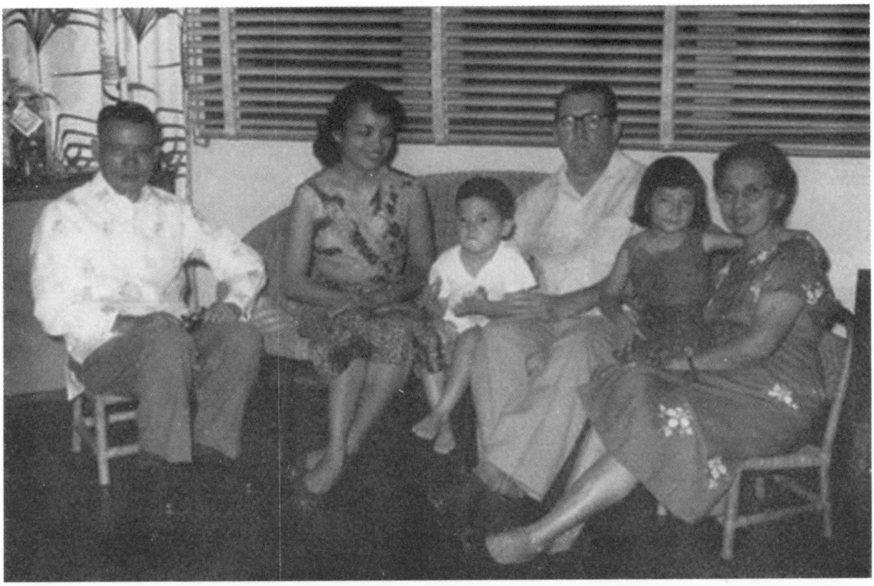

Jackson and Beltran family in Malate (1957).
L-R: Francisco Beltran (grandfather), Mary Vita Jackson (mother), James Jackson (brother), Lowell Monroe Jackson (father), Kristin Jackson, and Vitaliana Beltran (grandmother).

continued dancing as she enrolled at the Dance Arts Studio where she studied jazz under Julie Borromeo while also taking ballet in the same school. This was her first exposure to another way of dancing. Although Borromeo cast her as Wendy in *Peter Pan*, she realized her "technical weaknesses" in ballet compared to the other young ballerinas in her school.

Kristin's passion for dance was reignited after joining the summer modern dance workshops under Alice Reyes and Modern Dance Company (now Ballet Philippines) at the CCP. She felt she could be a dancer in another idiom besides ballet. Before joining the workshop that introduced her to modern dance, she felt ballet was still the career to pursue for any female dancer in Manila and elsewhere in the world at that time.

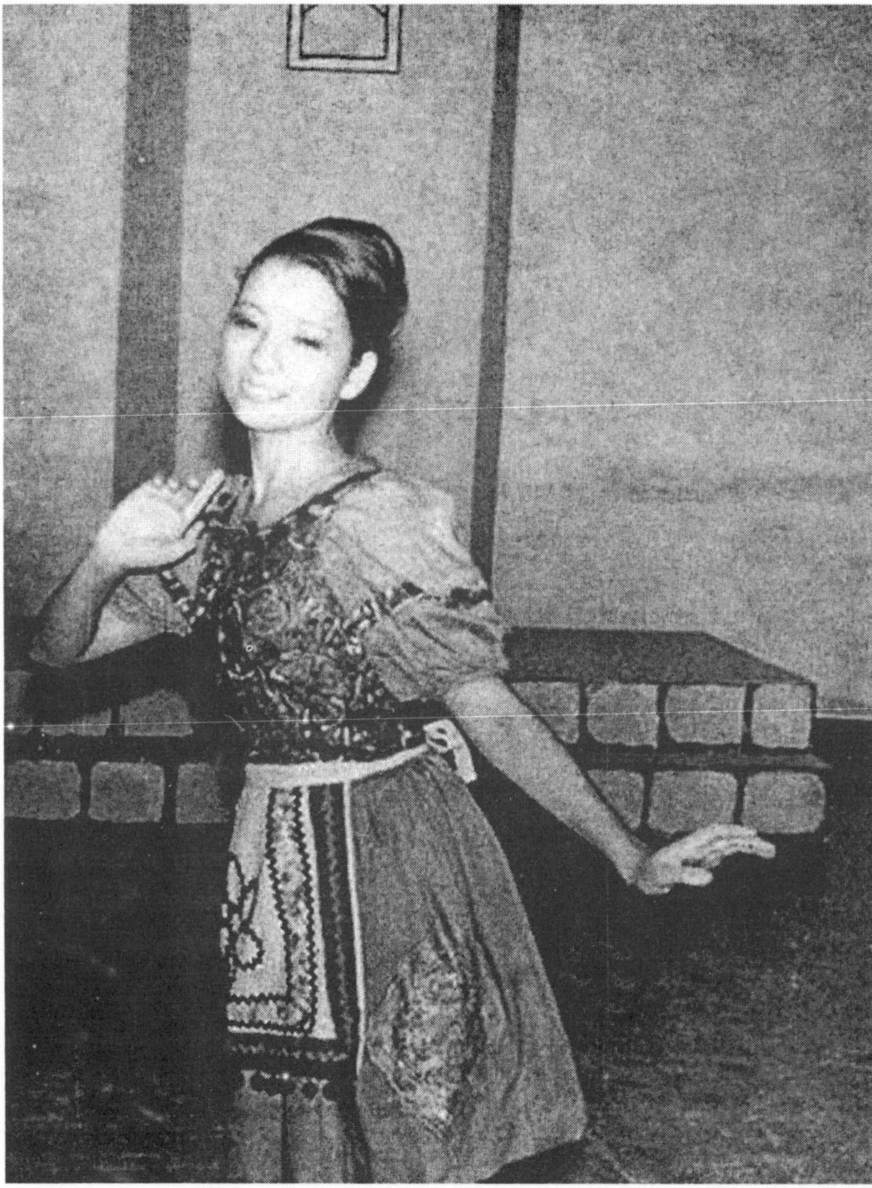

Kristin Jackson as Swanilda in Anita Kane's Philippine production of *Coppelia* (1966).

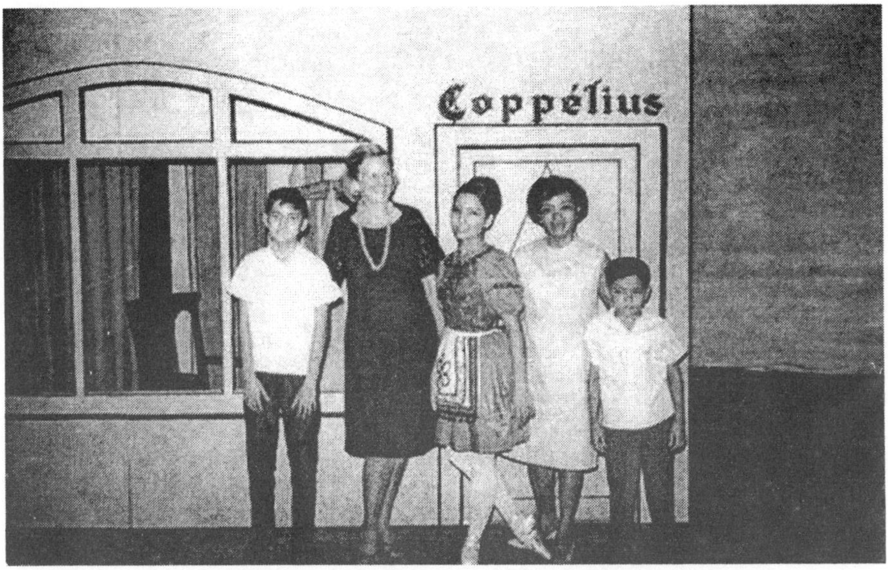

Family photo with Anita Kane on the set of *Coppelia* (1966).
L-R: James, Ms. Kane, Kristin, Mary Vita, and John.

The year was 1974 and Kristin, freshly graduating with a degree in editorial design from the UP College of Fine Arts, found more time to dance again. A year later, she left for New York with plans to continue studying dance, thinking that she would use it to teach dance later on in life. To financially support her dance classes, she worked as an assistant to an executive of a men's shirt company while diligently attending dance classes at night and during weekends.

At around this time, Kristin became involved on a part-time basis with the Reynaldo Alejandro Dance Theater (RADT), a modern dance company that used materials from Philippine themes and myths. Receiving encouraging responses from audiences and critics, she decided to leave her job in 1976 in order to commit to dance as a full-time profession. This proved to be a major shift in her dancing life, one which she calls a "decision of the heart," what with the reality of meager financial returns in pursuing dance as a career.

This was how she began dancing professionally these past thirty-six years and creating dances for the last fifteen years. "I feel most alive and complete when I am involved in dance,"[9] says Kristin of her decision and the ongoing commitment to pursue her life-long path and passion for a dance profession.

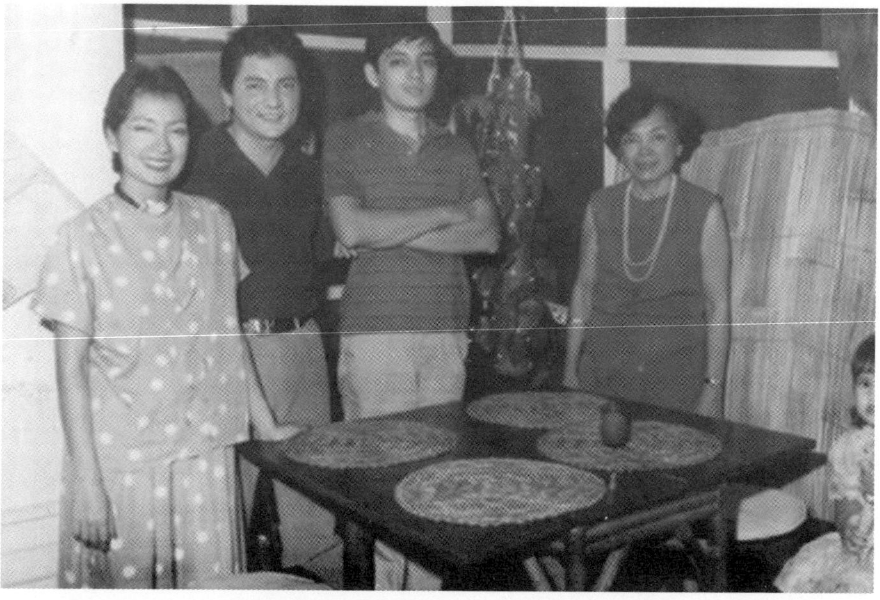

Jackson family in Pagasa, Q.C. (Christmas 1982).
L-R: Kristin, James, John, Mary Vita (mother), and Erin Campos, a family friend.

Presently an adjunct associate professor at the Queens College in New York, she has behind her a rich dance experience to share with a younger generation of dance students. After her stint in RADT, she danced with an international folk dance company called Allnations where she learned a repertoire of folk dances from Russia, Tahiti, Israel, and the Philippines, among others, as it toured to perform in the US and Asia. She was also invited to audition for the *King and I* Broadway production, a full-time paying job she accepted as she played Little Eva in the musical-dance in 1979 and again in 1981. In 1982, she joined the Chen and Dancers, a Chinese-American modern dance company. Here she learned to be "more open" as a dancer, and to fuse eastern and western dance traditions as the group toured Hong Kong and danced in New York.

One of her more prominent experiences was as a principal dancer and rehearsal director of the Laura Dean Dancers and Musicians from 1983 to 1987, which gave her the invaluable experience of performing on tour throughout the US, Canada, Europe and Japan. She managed to do this while completing an MFA in Dance at the New York University's Tisch School of the Arts.

Having developed expertise and proficiency in various movement styles, she finally set-up her own independent dance company in 1990 called Kristin Jackson Dance.

Minimalist movements

The clutter of movement styles and traditions one learns over time as a dancer and choreographer can create a sense of confusion in terms of defining one's own vocabulary in dance, and in developing a repertory different from those of a usually faddish dance world. Amidst the cross-cultural pressures of being Filipino-American and practicing dance in the culturally-diverse clime of New York City, Kristin had found for herself a clearly defined style of movement mainly characterized by stillness and uncluttered repetition. This minimalist aesthetic of quietness and calm in her movements is achieved by a composition of bare and basic movements repeated with simple variations throughout the performance. This goes against the grain of the relentless and restless showing-off of various movement styles and virtuoso techniques that is much deified in current American modern dance.

Kristin has refined a movement style that is quiet, almost akin to the contained and slow movements of the Chinese Tai'Chi and the Japanese Kabuki and Noh, but with the angularity and emotiveness of modern dance, and even traces of the grace and litheness of ballet. It was from her stint with the Laura Dean Dancers that she appreciated the movement idea that "less is more." This would further be affirmed in her trip to Japan in 1985 for her MA thesis research on Kabuki performances. In watching the Kabuki, she felt drawn to the "strong conveying-power of its purity and simplicity of movements." In 1996, she pursued this same fascination with Japanese movements as she studied the Noh dance and theater in Kyoto. In Noh dance, she noticed how bare and minimalist gestures could have immense signifying power:

> A branch could represent an entire tree, while a hand held over one eye could convey universal grief. The idea that "less is more" took on a deeper and more mysterious meaning. In becoming even more suggestive, I discovered that my dances were revealing more. It was an exciting discovery."[10]

Despite the clearly Asian, particularly Japanese, influence of her movement philosophy, she is still drawn to modern dance technique given its endless movement possibilities that can encompass practically any style. It is in the modern dance idiom that she has explored her mainly minimalist dance language as she is moved to distill movements to their "essence or core." She likens her choreographic process to "paring down a story to a few key phrases or words"—clearly reminiscent of the pithy verses of the Japanese haiku—which she thinks helped her to be more "focused and specific." Thus she would share her work philosophy:

> Since the creative life exists primarily on a subconscious level, one has to symbolically "shed" the conscious state, the familiar, the predictable, in order to find spontaneity and free one's self artistically. Only then does true discovery and creativity occur. I, not only start with a "clean" slate but I have to "die" a little to renew or reinvent myself.
>
> An idea for a dance can easily begin with a word, a gesture, an event or an image, then comes the harder task of transforming it into physical movement. I always try to find movement that comes from a human and instinctive place deep within, then develop it as fully as possible. The challenge and struggle is to stay honest and express myself simply and clearly. The risk of failure is always present, yet, like life, it is through adversity that knowledge is gained. (Choreographer's notes of Kristin Jackson in *Threshold*, Cultural Center of the Philippines, 1993)

Kristin's inner, nearly spiritual work philosophy, which she would instill into her dance-making, evokes the Zen Buddhist idea of emptiness and cleanliness of one's inner space as precondition to achieving a transcendent perfection in one's life and art. This focus on cleanliness of movements is in keeping with her process of non-linearity, which she also uses in her group choreographies known as "chance method," a process in dance that opposes the traditional linear logic of most Western theatrical and classical dances. Used by other modern choreographers such as Merce Cunningham, the "chance method" is a refreshing way of doing dance as it draws from non-traditional and non-imposing processes such as from the dancer's own experiences and improvisations.[11]

Moreover, this idea of authenticity to one's self, and the commitment not to succumb to the dance world vogue, was also sustained in her by Ruth Currier, her first choreography teacher at the NYU.[12] This further strengthened the characteristic quietness in her dance process, philosophy, and productions.

Inspired by reminiscences of Kristin father, *Field* (1982) captures the innocence and lightness of childhood as Kristin depicts herself playing with and letting go of a butterfly. A delicate and playful backbend ends with a gesture of catching a butterfly at her foot; this would be one of the most striking thematic movements interspersed throughout the dance.

> Thinking at first that *Field* was too personal and perhaps "out of fashion," Ruth Currier shared the most important advise with me, which gave me the courage to make this dance. She believed that one should never worry about what was trendy or popular when creating work. Rather, one should be true to oneself and create from your heart. There was no substitute for honesty and authenticity. The audience would always respond to honest work. It was precious advise that I have continued to be guided by.[13]

Still Waters (1990), a solo Kristin created in memory of her mother, is based on the Kalinga ritual of crossing a body of water as a final rite of mourning someone's death. In this piece that largely uses floor-bound movements, she gestures into washing her face and body with an imagined water before her, followed by the floor-work of kneeling movements where she fluidly goes forward and retreats back, suggesting the motion of going across tumultuous tides. Finally reaching the other side of the stage, she repeats the same ritual of washing face and body, this time marked with the conviction of having crossed the waters as she dignifiedly steps out from the trembling rivers back into solid ground. The literal and the metaphoric in her inner life and outer cultural landscape find meaningful convergence in this particular solo.

She elaborates further on the process she went through in doing this particular dance and how it was to continue on significantly as a personal metaphor and inspiration she uses for her journey in dance, especially with the loss of two souls that initially supported and nurtured her dancing:

> In 1984, while doing research for my thesis project, I came across a ritual practiced by the Kalinga people that involved "crossing a body of water" to signify the final stage in ending a period of mourning. In 1990, not realizing I would lose my mother two years later, I choreographed the solo *Still Waters* as a tribute to her strength and courage in facing my father's sudden death in 1966 and her capacity to transcend the loss and move on. Inspired by the Kalinga ritual, the image of crossing water became a metaphor for a recurring journey where as struggle ends, healing, renewal and transformation begin. This threshold, this "point of entering or beginning" is a place where I now find myself rediscovering life without the two people who gave it profound meaning, my parents. It is also where I believe my choreographic process starts.[14]

When the personal is political

The uncluttered, clear, and quietly emotive quality in Kristin's works is not only inscribed in her more personal/autobiographic choreographies, but also in a number of her other works that grapple with more pressing political issues. She considers *Pakiusap: A Mail Order Bride's Story* (1991) a significant work where she dwells on women's rights in the issue of Filipina mail-to-order brides.

> This is a piece I created as a tribute to women and the tragic choices or lack of choices they are faced with. The solo work traced back the journey of one of these women all the way to her wedding day. The piece was created in 1991 and 12 years later the problem continues to exist because of the continually troubled Philippine economy.[15]

In this evening-long dance/theater/installation work, a sole woman (originally danced by Kristin) in blouse and flowing skirt emerges from a makeshift Japanese wall-divider-cum-gift-box as an Asian man in black tuxedo comes out from the audience and presents her on stage. Like any true salesman, the well-dressed guy spouts catchy advertisement lines as: *Remember, if the woman in your life remains elusive, do something about it! Marry an Oriental woman, a woman for all time*! This text recited by the salesman was culled from excerpts of actual letters sent by mail order bride service organizations modified by Kristin and co-performer Ramon Hodel (who performed the Asian pimp) to suit theater conventions.

The music used, interestingly, is a collage of recordings from various Philippine popular culture sounds such as sounds from the local market—tricycle motors, voices of vendors, Pinoy pop songs—and ends with Kuh Ledesma's rendition of a *kundiman* similarly titled *Pakiusap*. The Filipina's gaze is downcast all throughout the dance, expressing submissiveness. She would gesture into movements her culturally stereotyped attributes such as *hinhin* (demure)—shown through graceful arm and leg moves as she coyly sits on the floor—and *sipag* (industriousness) which is shown in a pantomimic gesture of her as a scrupulous market vendor, selling her wares amidst sounds of haggling customers, raging jeepneys and tricycles, and other sounds from the local flea market. The final scene speaks poignantly of the bride's lament, when after dancing to the *kundiman*—a song pleading for love—she changes to a bridal gown and is encased once more inside the makeshift divider. As the lights dim, only her silhouette is seen, with her head cast down and one arm reaching upwards, as if gesturing against the tragedy of her containment in the package.

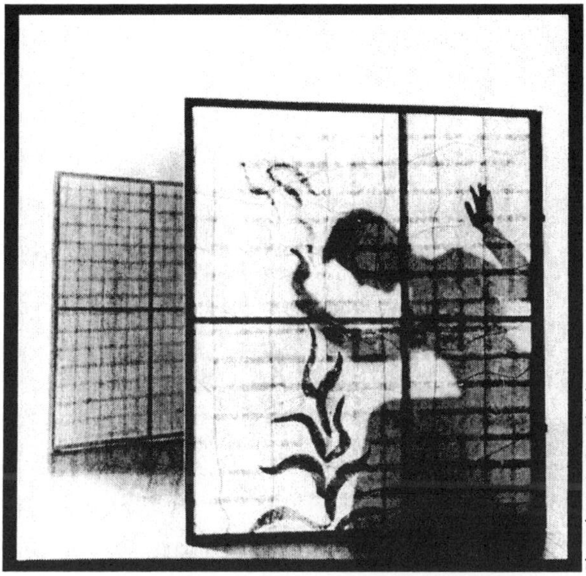

Photo by Lois Geenfield

Pakiusap (1991), choreographed and performed by Kristin Jackson at Dia Center for the Arts in September 1991.

Another powerful politically inspired work is *Arctic Archipelago* (1988), a male solo performed with a recitation of Luis H. Francia's poem of the same title that depicts in elegiac free verse the atrocities of the Marcos regime. Kristin would deliver the poem while a male dancer perilously walks and moves atop and around a wooden bench, approximating the Filipino festive folk dance *sayaw sa bangko,* but this time using it as a parody for the restlessness of a nation deeply mired in the injustices of a dictatorship.

One work that distinctly merges her personal and political cross-cultural experiences is *In their Shoes* (1998). It is a multimedia work developed from an earlier solo called *In Her Shoes* (1996) which revolves around stories of war based on her family's experience of poverty and humane friendship with Japanese hospital workers during the Japanese occupation of the Philippines in World War II. The work's most recent version, commissioned by the Colden Center for the Performing Arts, was a collaboration with Filipino poet Luis H. Francia who directed the oral histories and testimonies of over thirty Filipino and Japanese war survivors. Rich Billay did the videography, Keiko Fujie the original music, and dance was by Kristin Jackson Dance. In the video, Kristin shares the testimony her mother—who during the war was a nurse—passed on to her as a child. It told how she and her two brothers shared only one pair of shoes during the war, and the surprise of unsolicited help from supposed enemies—the Japanese health workers at St. Luke's Hospital. With her mother gone by the time of the dance production, it was Kristin's maternal uncle, Salvador Beltran, who retold in the video the anecdote about the shoes. The dance was choreographed as a group performance, with Kristin opening the act by quietly standing in front of a pair of shoes, putting them on, and moving on to dance as she recited: *Sana nagtanong pa ako / Ng mas maraming kuwento / Habang nandito pa sila / Hindi ko dapat malimutan.*

A female Asian dancer from the opposite side of the stage mirrored her moves, reciting the same lines in English ("I wish I had asked / for more stories / While they're still here / I mustn't forget") while a group of other dancers slowly entered to interpret the narrative amidst the background of the videotaped narratives.

Kristin and her musical collaborator Keiko Fujie wrote in their program notes about their families' similar experiences of war's more human face:

> In our countries, most of what was written about war focused on tragedy, with little evidence of more human and hopeful encounters. Upon discovering that our families' stories revealed more compassionate relationships, we realized the importance and power of sharing these stories—as well as encouraging new stories to be told. By making these stories the focus of our collaborative work, we hope to honor the memories of our families and our countries, allowing future generations to find healing and closure. (*In their Shoes* program notes, 1998)

Kristin's inclination to show what is unpredictable, what is least talked about and known in the mainstream of culture, and that which is also deeply drawn from her roots, particularly her family's experiences in the Philippines, is particularly revealed in *In Their Shoes*.

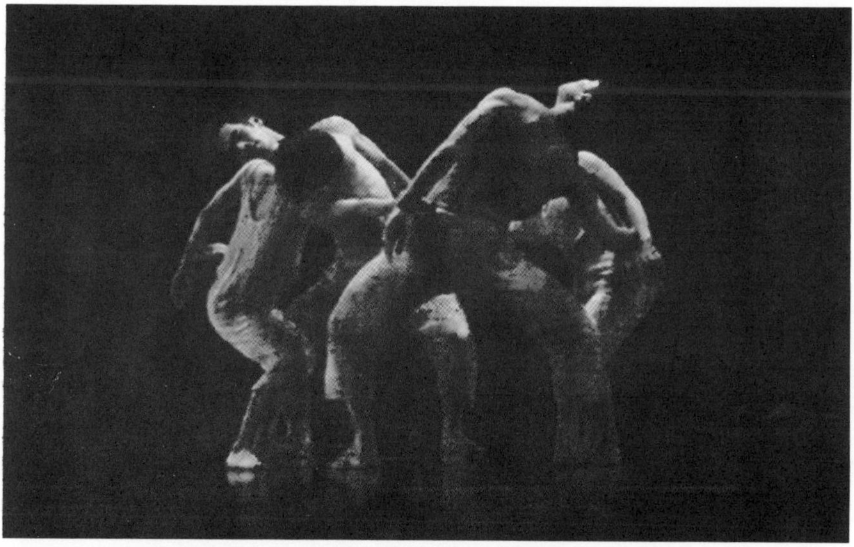

Photo by Ellen Crane

In Their Shoes choreography by Kristin Jackson (1998) at
Colden Center for the Performing Arts, NY.
L-R: Kazu Nakamura, Nami Yamamoto, Chan Koo Paik, and Jennifer Chin.

Other collaborative efforts similar to this also characterize most of Kristin's professional relations with other New York-based independent artists, theater companies, and cause-oriented groups. She has also been commissioned to choreograph for theater productions, mostly those with Asian-American or Filipino-American themes, such as for Ma-Yi Theater Company's *The Romance of Magno Rubio* (2002), a work based on Filipino activist-writer Carlos Bulosan's novel on being a Filipino in America; the National Asian American Theater Company's *Adventures of Momotaro* (1989), *The Stronger* (1991), *The House of Bernarda Alba* (2000); and Gabriela Women's Network in *Apat na Hangin* (1992), a duet based on relationships between Filipina mothers and daughters.

Despite being political and culturally specific, her works still articulate ideas of "transcendence" and "universality." And although aware of her racial grounded-ness (as Filipino-Irish-American, as she would sometimes describe her lineage), she still thinks of herself mainly as an artist whose works can "transcend boundaries" and gather appreciation from audiences regardless of nationality or gender.

> I believe that these intersections [of race and gender] exist inherently in anyone's art. It is what makes the artist unique. However much I am proud to be a woman of Philippine-Irish-American descent born and raised in Manila, I still like to think of myself as an artist first. My personal experiences and influences will always be consciously or subconsciously palpable in my work. Whether I draw from my experiences growing up in the Philippines or my more recent experiences in New York, what is most important is that my work be universally relevant. Yes, perhaps I am more naturally drawn to gender issues and ongoing questions about my identity with works about the mail order bride problem to the Marcos dictatorship to an exploration of my Irish ancestry

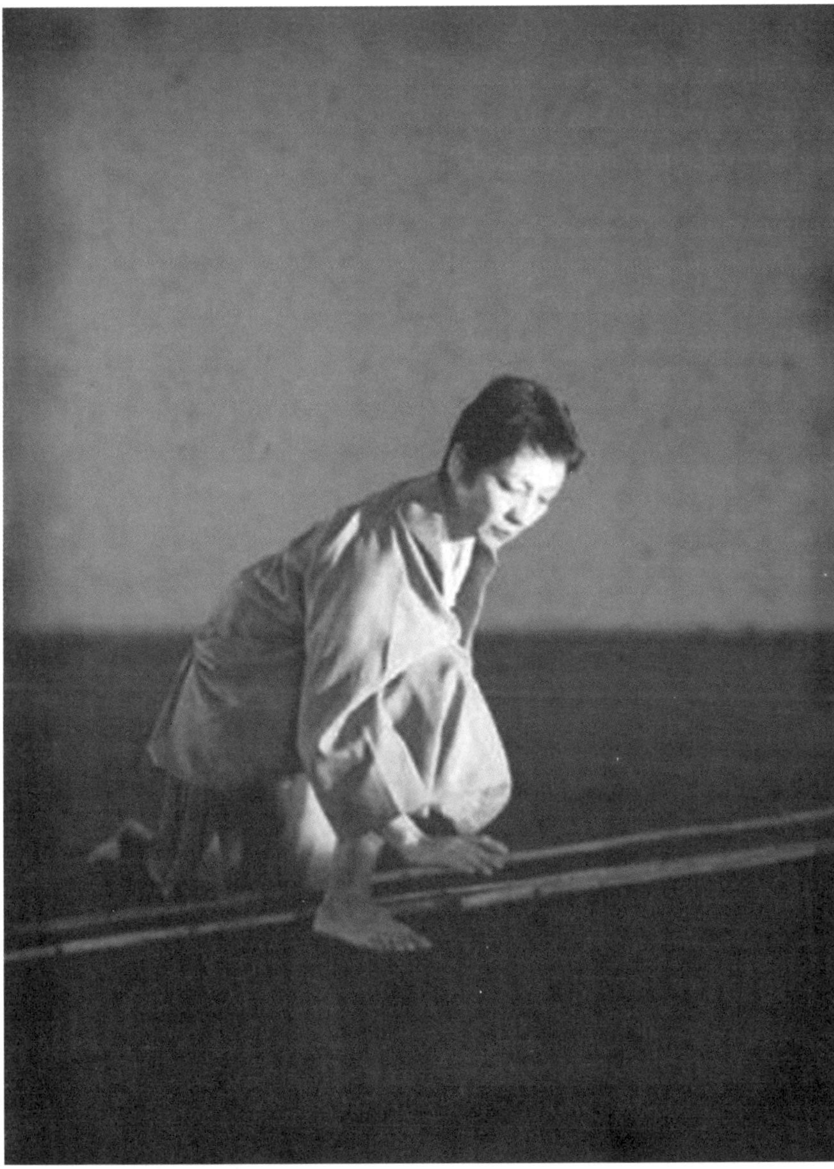

Photo by Hiroyuki Ito

A Clearing (1998), choreographed and performed by Kristin Jackson at Joyce SoHo, NY in January 2001.

> since this is my experience. Yet, I would like to think that these subject matters are as relevant to both female and male audience members of all nationalities. The idea once more of "transcending boundaries" is what has made dance so important and special to me all these years.[16]

Kristin, however, remains cognizant of gender differentiation and the very specific role of women in the dance world. She, for instance, mentions how women have brought "great humanity to the art form" despite social expectations for them "to compete and be more aggressive in a man's world." Similarly, she observes that despite the more egalitarian relationships in modern dance companies in America, women still have to work and rehearse more than their male counterparts for the same amount of money. This is largely because there are fewer male dancers who are

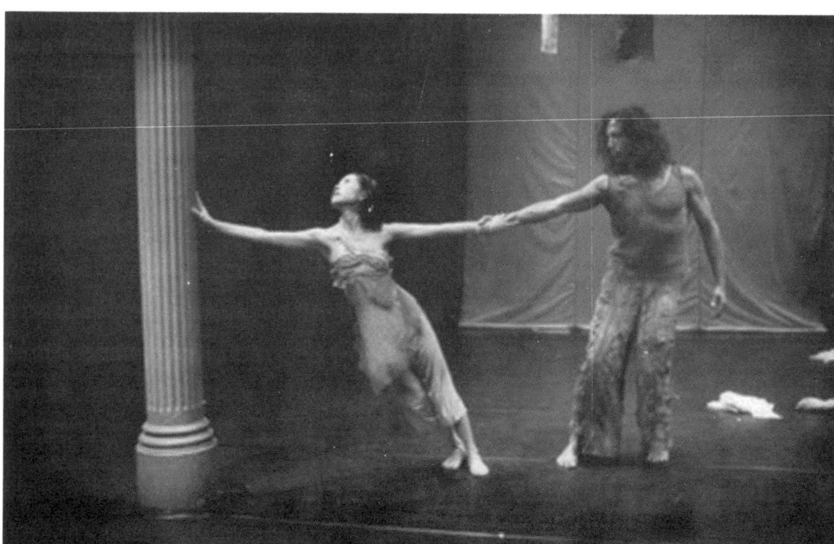

Photo by Hiroyuki Ito

Wind (2002), choreographed by Kristin Jackson and performed by Kuan Hui Chew and Rodger Belman at the Mulberry St. Theater in June 2002, NY.

therefore more in demand such that they are eventually preferentially treated in established dance institutions.

With the passion to share of herself and her ideas through the medium of dance as a personalized, and often politicized, art form, Kristin has found audiences in various loft and theater spaces in New York City and Boston, in Manila's Cultural Center of the Philippines (mainly under Ballet Philippines' Neo-Filipino series), and much recently at the UP Abelardo Hall.

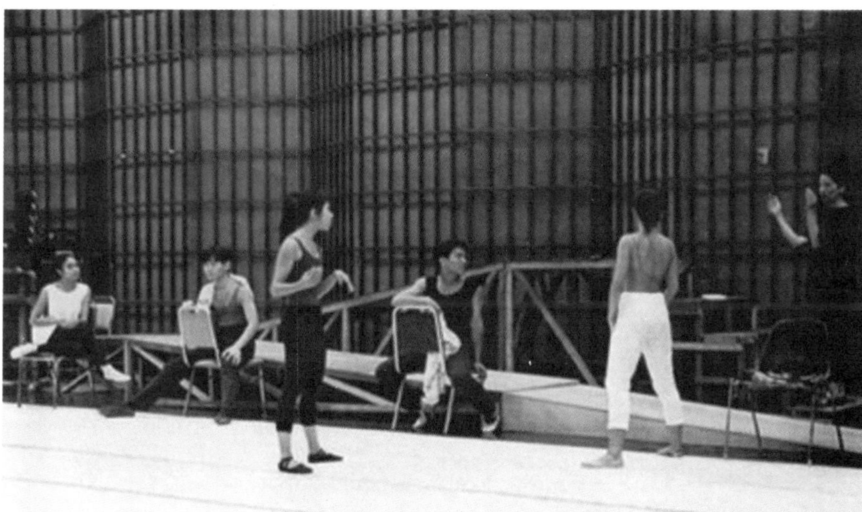

Rehearsal for the 1993 Choreographer's Showcase with Ballet Philippines dancers at CCP. L-R: Wendy Panginiban, Anton Perez, Annie Divinagracia, Elmer Domdom, Isabel Gregorio, and Kristin Jackson

Egalitarian dance practice

Kristin realizes both the pleasures and perils of going independent. She mainly appreciates the sense of autonomy in having greater control over her ideas for her dance productions and the entire creative process that goes with it, which in a dance company is usually infringed upon by the artistic director, choreographer, and even by its board of trustees. The downside of it, however, is that she has to wear too many hats, from fundraiser, to director, choreographer, and performer all at the same time. This is made no easier by the lack of funding available for independent artists and the stiff competition for the meager funding resources when they are made available in New York.

But it is with her intense dedication, and the vision to create and look at dance in other ways, that she is able to make a mark in her independent dance practice overseas. This is seen in the way she regards her audience, empowering them as her own collaborators, at the same time maintaining her commitment to go beyond what is simply predictable and pleasing:

> I also like to think of the audience as another one of my collaborators in the sense that they are "active" participants in the realization of my work. Although I try to be sensitive to their needs by not making my work too long or too personal, I don't believe that the audience should define how I choreograph. *My intent is to challenge them and make them see movement in new ways, not cater to what they are accustomed to seeing.* (E-mail correspondence, March 22, 2004; italics mine)

As a dance teacher at Queens College, her pedagogy also transcends the deeply ingrained master-apprentice hierarchy in traditional/ mainstream dance education and practice, as it does the structures of most dance conservatories locally and abroad. The same teaching philosophy of democratizing dance informs her working relationship with her co-dancers at Kristin Jackson Dance.

> I look at each student as an individual and try to honor his or her uniqueness. I have had much practice with this at Queens College since this is a Liberal Arts College where many of the students don't necessarily go into performing careers but are still interested in learning about it. Some students may have had adequate dance experience while others haven't—and they are all in the same class. Even though I structure the class based on the subject that I am teaching, my priority is to adapt it to the needs of the students. I also believe in a democratic style of teaching. I provide structure and guidance as a means of helping the students find their own way of learning. I don't believe in threatening the students to make then learn. I encourage them to take personal responsibility for their learning. I am merely their "guide." This can be a challenge, of course, if a student is not mature enough to handle this kind of responsibility. But in my experience, except for those few exceptions, it has been more rewarding for both myself and the students to use this approach.
>
> I choreograph in the same way. I have an egalitarian relationship with my dancers. I value their suggestions and contributions. They are artists, who I respect and honor. A dance would not exist without them. As a result, I have developed life-long friendships with many of them. Without doubt, this has been the best part of being a choreographer. (Email correspondence, March 22, 2004)

Working with her independent group, Kristin has mainly worked with Asian-American dancers and a few Caucasian dancers whose ages range from mid-20s to early 40s. Most of them are choreographers and teachers like Kristin, which makes them more attuned to the creative process of dance. When working for theater groups, however, she finds her process more collaborative and non-imposing as she merely sees herself as a "guide" facilitating what the theater actors can express in movement.

In her productions, Kristin usually only involves from one to five dancers, depending on the requirements of a dance project. Keeping her cast small also ensures that she is able to honor her financial commitment to pay the dancers for rehearsals, which is not always a practice in New York City and elsewhere, besides paying for their performances. She also respects her time commitments to rehearsals by beginning on time and not extending beyond 1 to 2 hours, again a counter practice to the usual company rehearsals that go on up to midnight.[17]

This commitment as a choreographer and artistic director would show her sensitivity to the economic needs of dancers, and a deep sense of respect for their time, having observed and gone through the less-than-humane circumstances that dancers experience in their careers. Embedded deeply beyond the issue of respect for time and financial commitment is how she has built her interactions with her dancers around the more prized values of collegiality, professionalism, and mutual trust, which are often wanting in traditional companies where dancers are beholden to the egotistical and sometimes abusive whims of an overbearing artistic director. The life-long friendships that she has formed with her dancers is one that she would describe as "rewarding and stimulating" as she considers and treats them as "peers and mature collaborators."

This same ethic of collaboration and peer-exchange was what dance majors at the College of Music found in Kristin during her stint as lecturer. Angel Lawenko of UP Dance Company especially found inspiring how Kristin facilitated the creation of a collaborative piece called *Banwa* (community) to the ethnic-inspired music of Jonas Baes. It turned out to be a meaningful personal and collective piece for their group who expressed their sense of community as young dancers placed in their individual and larger contexts as university students. In this process, the students/dancers

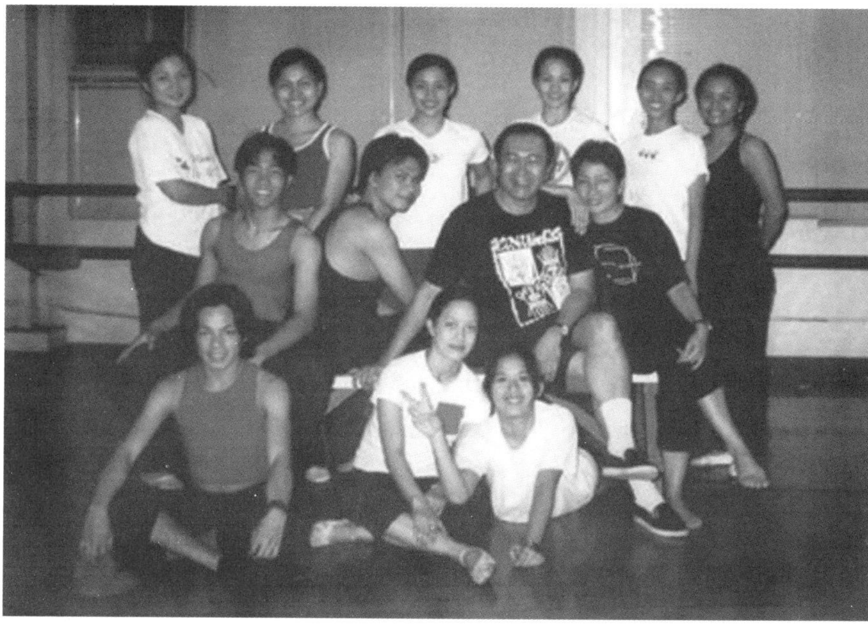

Kristin Jackson in a rehearsal for *Banwa* in 2003 with Steve Villaruz and the UP Dance Company.
L-R: (Back line standing) Joyce Comia, Ava Villanueva, Jantu Revilla, Jay-Ann Tensuan, Bea Puno
(Middle line seated on bench) Brizel Maribay, Wally Tuyan, Professor Steve Villaruz, Kristin Jackson
(Front line seated on floor) Ernest Hojilla, Marielle Alonzo, Yvonne Torres

were asked to answer several questions about their dancing, mainly how they began dancing and who influenced them in the process. Personal memories of their provinces, familial affinities were conjured in their dancing. They were asked to transform their verbal answers into colored drawings which they then turned into movements that made up the whole dance.

A strong sense of groundedness, almost humility, amidst the vast yet differentiated experiences that are woven around Kristin's life and those around her, have made her—whether as dancer, choreographer, or teacher—one who is self-disciplined and committed to dance as art, while remaining sensitive to signs and signals from the various worlds that she would straddle, and still learn to begin from there. As she would meaningfully impart in one of her local performances:

> So I continue to hone my craft, remain observant of life around me, stay tuned to my inner voice and know that the next time I walk into an empty studio I will be able to step into the "water" and begin again. (Choreographer's notes of Kristin Jackson in *Threshold,* 1993)

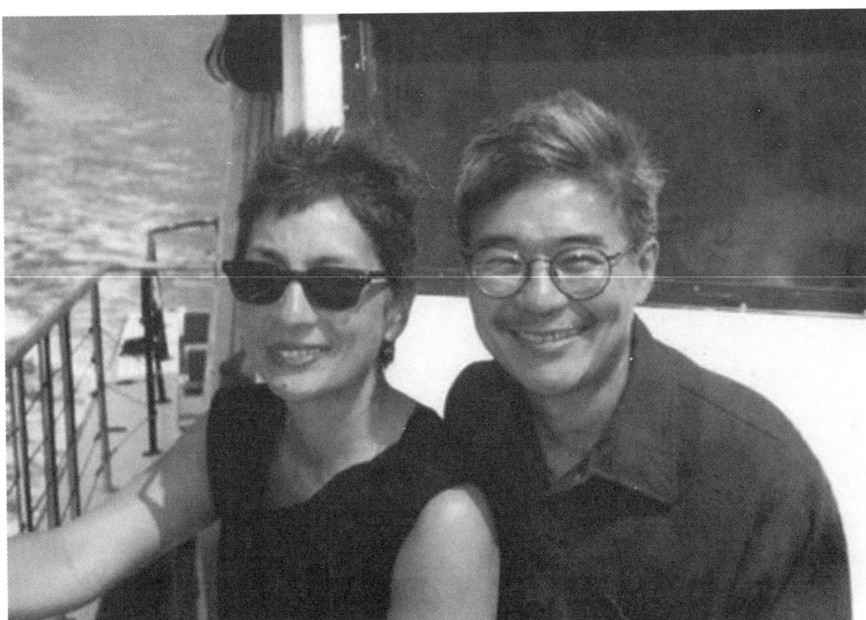

Kristin Jackson and husband Eric Achacoso dolphin watching in Savannah, Georgia in 2004.

Agnes Locsin: Neoethnic Negotiations

Way before I personally met Agnes, I read a critical essay by Sally Ann Ness titled *Originality in the Postcolony: Choreographing the Neoethnic Body of Philippine Ballet* (1997), which extensively critiques her neo-ethnic work *Igorot*—by far her most celebrated, and also her most controversial, piece. I had also noticed this near canonical status given to *Igorot* when I saw the change of logo in the Ballet Philippines programs which I kept through the years as an occasional CCP audience. The logo, which before showed an image of a male dancer's upper torso in a leaping position, had been changed to that of an *Igorot* priestess performing balletic legwork of *a la seconde attitude*, her arms outstretched and hands flexed in a Cordilleran bird-mimicking gesture, her gaze directed downwards (see photo). It was, apparently, a pose taken from *Igorot*. I found it extremely inviting to offer my own reading of the sources and influences that could be reckoned from the logo; this later became the topic of my final paper[18] for a graduate course. It was already several years after *Igorot*'s premiere, so I had to watch the dance in a video at the CCP library in the process of writing the said paper.

Ballet Philippines logo.

In doing the research paper for *Igorot,* I also interviewed Christine Maranan—one of the dancers who learned and performed *Igorot* under Agnes' artistic directorship—then freshly resigned from Ballet Philippines (BP), and now a freelance dance artist. At that time, year 2000, Christine was also collaborating on a production with Myra Beltran called *Daughters of Necessity: Women Solos in Dance.* "Independent dancing" was still a hazy construction in the Philippine cultural landscape then, but was undeniably already moving quite palpably in the air.

I carried these impressions of Agnes as I visited her in her home some three years later. She is now decidedly on her own in Davao City, low-key and resigned after a fourteen-year stint with Ballet Philippines, but still teaching and creating dances in her mother's studio. This is what I make of our conversations, as she walked me through stories inside a library of personal and family albums, memorabilia, program notes, a chest of video tapes of her works, and files of yet unarranged articles about her dances which she has compiled over the years. Most of these collected things have grown brown and dusty with time, and she loudly wishes to find time to work on these, as she remains busy teaching dance, besides gardening and being company to her seventy-eight-year-old mother.

Home-grown roots

Agnes Dakudao Locsin recalls watching at 4 pm everyday their family sala turn into a dance studio, which her mother Carmen D. Locsin would regularly set-up, primarily as an avocation, and secondly to supplement the family income. Agnes, born in 28 September 1957, is the youngest in the brood of five boys and one other girl, Bing, who is the eldest of the Locsin children.

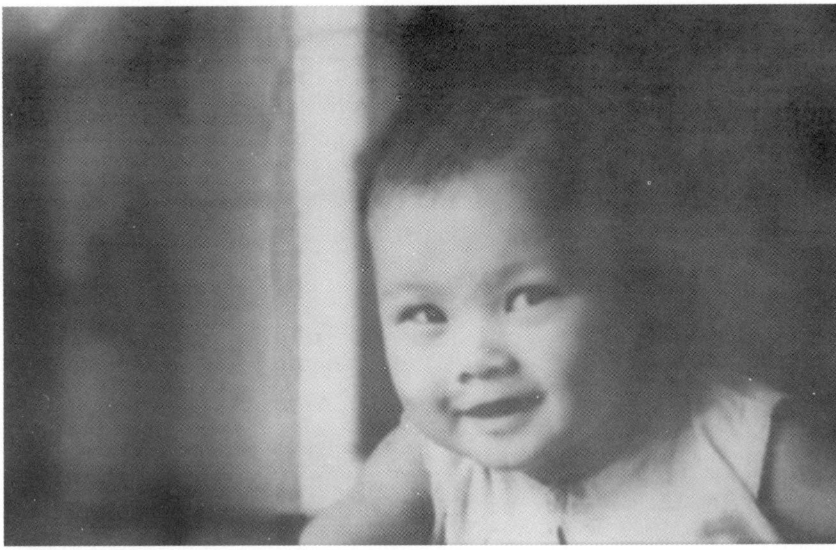

Photo by Jose Locsin

Agnes at 6 months old.

"To get to know me, one has to first to get to know my mother,"[19] Agnes would intimate of her dancing life's affinity with her mother's own love affair with dance. Mommy Carmen, as Mrs. Locsin is fondly called by dance habitués of Davao City, pioneered the first ballet school in Davao, circa 1947. The school, now called the Locsin Dance Workshop, still exists, making it at sixty years the oldest ballet school in the Philippines. Today, it is no longer a sala-cum-studio, but a two-studio dance school within the Locsin compound along Davao's Quirino Avenue.

Mommy Carmen, as a high schooler at St. Scholastica in Manila, took her first dance training in ballet with Leonor Orosa Goquingco, who belongs to the first generation of ballet teachers and choreographers in the country. Ricardo Cassell and Anita Kane were also her teachers.

"She said she could have been a dancer herself but instead she fell in love with a young photographer named Jose Severino Locsin, my father, and danced the dance of family," Agnes wrote in an article celebrating the fiftieth year since her mother first taught ballet in Davao. The affair that cut short Mommy Carmen's prospects of being a dancer happened during the Filipino-Japanese war, when the two eloped as young teenagers, and finally settled to raise a family in Davao City. Later, the young Carmen went to Manila to refresh herself with ballet classes taught by various teachers. In the mid-1960s, during summer vacations, she started bringing the young Agnes to take dance classes with her in various dance schools in Manila.

Mommy Carmen recalls that at the age of two-and-a-half years, Agnes was already insisting on joining her ballet classes. Before she started, one-third of the early attendees of their ballet classes were their female relatives; later, even her nephews attended until they were in sixth grade.

Agnes recalls how the whole family was mobilized around Mommy Carmen's teaching and setting-up of dance recitals: "It used to be a family affair. *Sa* recital, *kasali kami lahat*: my brother was in charge of the lights, hall preparation, some of them performed and partnered the girls. I and my sister would dance. My father was the photographer, aside from handling the pre-production and ticket sales. The dance school was the family's source of income, because my dad was underpaid." Agnes' cousin, Jesse Paspe, designed the stage for their recitals.

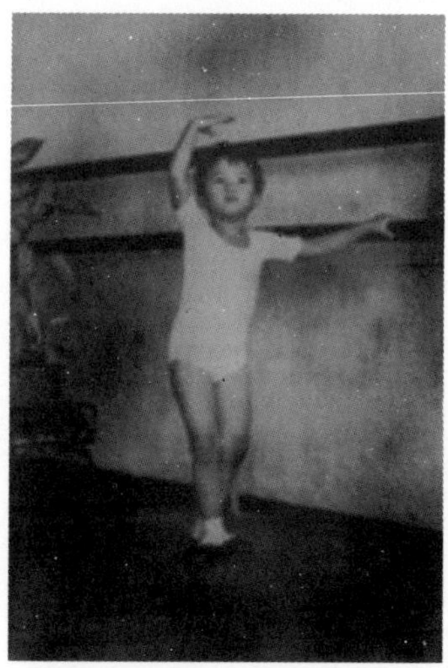

Photo by Jose Locsin

Agnes at two and a half years old in the Locins' sala/studio in Claveria St., Davao City.

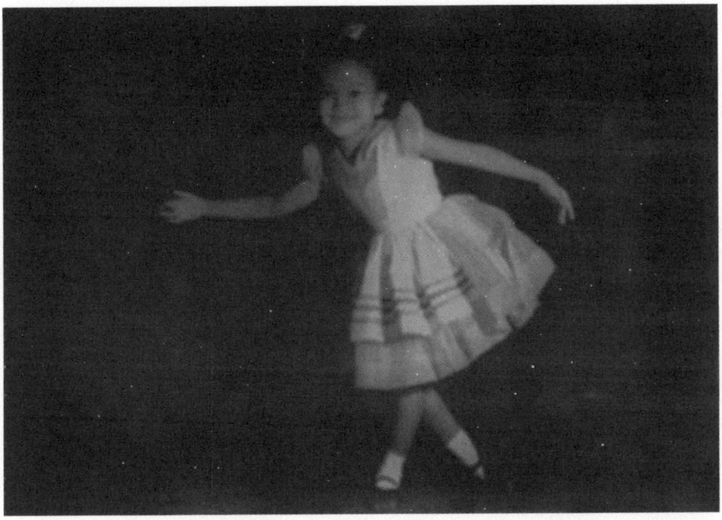

Photo by Jose Locsin

Agnes as Jill, Jack's partner, recital dance in 1965.
Photo session with her dad, Jose Locsin.

In recollecting this, Agnes pointed out that no one forced her into dancing, saying that dance was practically her entire life. "I knew I wouldn't be a bank teller, a housewife, or a lawyer. I practically breathed dance."

After spending one semester at the University of Santo Tomas as an architecture student—thinking she would follow the footsteps of her uncle, National Artist Leandro Locsin—she realized that she missed setting up dances in her mother's studio. Writing her father about this homesickness, she was sent back home and decided to take up English at the Ateneo de Davao. It was at this time that she met fellow students and artists in the university, musician Joey Ayala and writer Al Santos, who became her frequent collaborators in her future choreographic works. Agnes, however, mostly credits her brother Michael, then a graduate student at Stanford, for convincing their mother about the idea of her joining him to pursue a master's degree abroad. "I was very simple-minded, I did not have big dreams. I just enjoyed choreographing shows in my mom's studio and in the university dance group. When my brother brought up the idea, I just said, 'Hmm, that must be interesting'."

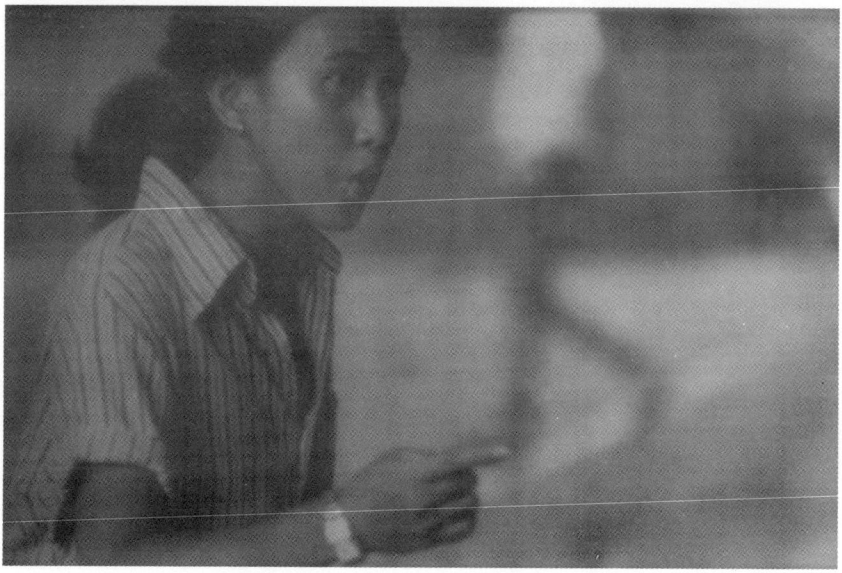

Photo by Jose Locsin

Agnes at nineteen years old, directing a dance concert for a school organization in Ateneo De Davao University.

With several dance productions under her belt,[20] off she went to Ohio State University to take an MA in Dance. She attributes it to sheer "luck" that several years after returning home from graduate studies in America, the local dance world, particularly the CCP's Ballet Philippines, was open and ready for another new choreographer.

Born to an old landed family from Negros that later migrated to Davao, Agnes found it easy to pursue and sustain dance as a career that generally did not reward one financially. "It was because the *copras* still fetched a high price at that time—that was how I got sent to the US," she relates, recalling the farming and real estate business that Mommy Carmen had inherited from her father, Dr. Santiago Dakudao, Sr.

It was within this general context that Agnes found herself developing into a dancer, and later, a choreographer.

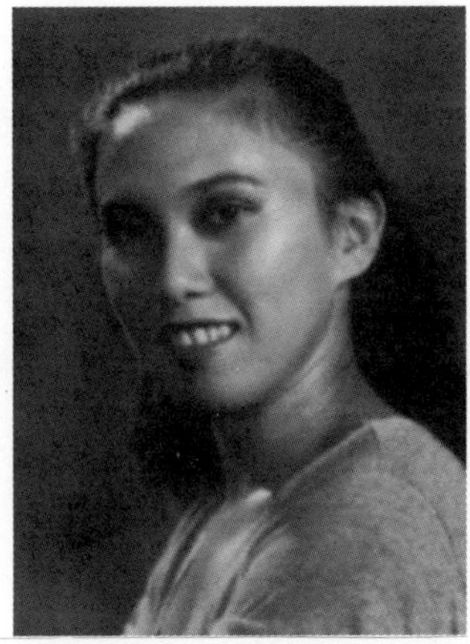

Photo by Jose Locsin

Agnes at twenty-three years old, just arrived from the US as a new graduate of dance at Ohio State University.

Choreographic beginnings

Agnes was already fond of directing shows during her teenage years. In her personal library, one of the first things she showed me was a page from her photo album which had among others her piece of writing as a fifteen-year-old senior student narrating her experience of directing a high school production in her junior and senior years.

Besides the experience of leadereship at school productions, Agnes also developed the aptitude and skill to direct group productions in her mother's studio during dance recitals. Her mother perennially tasked her to choreograph for their annual recitals, Filipino-themed dances, which Mommy Carmen kept in her repertoire as instilled in her by her former teacher Orosa-Goquingco (whose dance works were themselves largely Filipino in theme and narrative). Whenever Mommy Carmen left town, the young Agnes handled her mother's ballet classes, together with two more senior dancers. This experience gave her a sense of leadership in teaching and choreographing groups of dancers, preparing her to take on more challenging roles in the future.

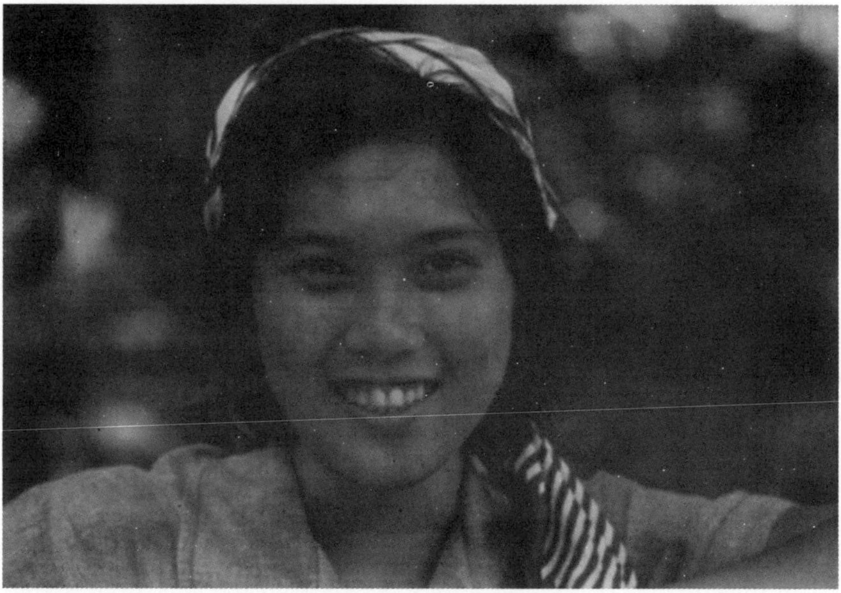

Agnes at sixteen years old.

Starting independently

Although to the public's mind, it was only very recently that Agnes became an independent dance practitioner—four years to be exact since she left Ballet Philippines—she says that her roots in independent dance production started when she choreographed works in her mother's dance studio. Indeed, her beginnings in the dance world were very much self-sustained and home-grown, as she learned the trade of crafting dances from watching her mother and sister in their family studio, and taking classes under her mother: "My mother was my only regular teacher of dance in my youth. She gave me such a hard time that she often scolded me. She was very demanding. I can see that she handled me with tenderness and sternness too. But she did succeed in instilling in me the discipline of dance. Her greatest desire was to see me dance. Unfortunately, I became a choreographer instead."

Agnes had merely learned from seeing her mother choreographing all the pieces in their school recitals until she was assigned that directorship role as she grew more mature in her mother's trade. Her elder sister Bing brought jazz and tap into the school after training abroad. And it was under her that Agnes learned these two forms of dances, from which she also took inspiration in her future works.

"We love to teach. *Ang naiwan na lang ngayon* is *yung* love *namin sa sayaw*. No matter what, this child has to dance well. My mom screams, and is strict. We're exactly the same when teaching is concerned," Agnes shares with a laugh, saying how just watching her mother teach dance was a whole education unto itself. She says her mother was even stricter in teaching her as she used to carry a stick for slacking legs in ballet class. "But the stick disappeared 30 years ago," she fondly remembers this strong sense of discipline and commitment to dance infused into her by her mother.

The Locsin Dance Workshop, though known in Davao, remained low-key and non-commercial, and was almost unknown and marginal to Manila-centered culturatis at that time, and even up to the present, making it a school independently run wholly by the Locsin family.

Returning home at age twenty-three and with an MA in dance, Agnes took on the artistic directorship of the Locsin Dance Workshop. She danced and independently produced dances for the studio until she was twenty-eight. She would be the school's artistic consultant from thereon even as she decided to apply as faculty of the CCP Dance School in Manila. Getting into the institutional ranks of Ballet Philippines, Agnes became the lone teacher of modern dance, given her exposure abroad. At the same time, she was also faculty of the UP Dance program, PETA (Philippine Educational

Theatre Association) and Tanghalang Pilipino, and artistic consultant of the Jazz Tap Center.

However, her longest standing job was at the CCP where she rose from faculty to Artistic Director, first of its junior resident company Ballet Philippines II (BP II) from 1989 to 1990, and later of Ballet Philippines itself—BP II's mother company composed of more senior professional dancers—from 1994 to 1996. Three years hence she served as chief choreographer of the company. "It was *lagare* all the way," Agnes says. "I was teaching anything and everything to support myself. I had to ride buses and jeepneys to economize. I had to live with relatives who provided me with free board and lodging. I really worked hard to get to where I am now. *Pinaghirapan ko talaga* and I am proud that I rose from the ranks in the CCP on my own merits."[21] She decided to resign in 1999, ending a productive fourteen-year stint with the CCP's main resident dance company.

As the then lone modern dance teacher at CCP,[22] Agnes relates how difficult it was to get dancers to take her classes because classical ballet was still valued more by the institution and the dance world. Agnes' technique in enlisting students to her classes, she fondly recollects, was by befriending them first so they wouldn't turn down her invitation to take her classes. "In later years, I got them addicted to modern dance," she proudly says. True enough, BP now holds one of the most eclectic modern dance choreographies in the country, and Agnes was very much behind that history. To date, even after Agnes left the institution, she has left a vast body of modern or contemporary works. In fact, six out of the twelve dances in BP's current repertoire were choreographed by Agnes. These are *Babaylan* (1994), *La Revolucion Filipina* (1996), *Igorot* (1994), *Taong Talangka* (1994), *Moriones* (1994), and *Salome* (1998).

Threads of the neo-ethnic

Even before making it to Manila and making a name in the mainstream institutional dance world, Agnes had already independently produced quite a number of works in Davao. For the Ateneo-based Terpsichoreans, she choreographed *Carmen* (1977), *Sisa* (1978), *Ligawan* (1978), and *Lupe* (1978). *Sa Bundok ng Apo* (1977), a rock opera based on Bagobo myths and legends, was her first collaboration with Al Santos as director and Joey Ayala as musician, and also one of the first stirrings of the neo-ethnic works she would later be known for. After returning from her studies abroad, she also independently produced, choreographed, and danced for their family studio's performing group Locsin Dance Ensemble. Some of these productions were *Teresa* (1982)—commissioned by the Carmelites of Zamboanga—a modern dance piece on the life of St. Therese of Avila, and *Katrina* (1982), a modernized *pas de deux* based on Shakespeare's *Taming of the Shrew*. Both were performed on tour in Davao, Cagayan de Oro, and Zamboanga—an early mark for the young Agnes as a dance artist.

The decision to choreograph full time, she says, was not conscious but began in her college days. "If I decided then to concentrate on dancing, nobody would be there to choreograph or direct shows. And I wanted to put up shows because I felt incomplete without them. I never even bothered to think that I could be a better dancer than a choreographer. I figured I had more value as director, choreographer and producer. Anyway there were other good dancers to work with."

Once, while doing *Teresa,* she overheard an audience saying that it was *swapang* (selfish) to see her always the *bida* (hero) in her own choreography. Taking the comment seriously, she began to see that there were indeed other good dancers that she can work with, and that she was better at leading and directing shows. Mommy Carmen had always wanted to see Agnes dance, but Agnes chose a path similar to her mother's—that of taking care of other younger dancers and teaching them the discipline of dance. Agnes found it to be more enjoyable than repeating a repertoire of dances as a performer. After her performances for Denisa Reyes' *Asong Ulol,* and Enrico Labayen's *Sabel,* she decided never to perform as a dancer again but just choreograph full time.

It was when she went to Europe in 1987 to take and explore modern dance techniques further that she felt all the more inclined to find out what was to set her brand of choreography apart. There, she found every dance company already very proficient in ballet and modern. Searching for ways to make her choreography as a Filipina be different, she took a choreographic project for the Le Petite Theatre Amsterdam and chose to do one based on her past fieldwork and dance research on Igorot culture. It was, ironically, for this foreign dance company that her most famous neo-ethnic ballet work *Igorot* was first choreographed and premiered, even before it was taken on by BP in its repertoire.

"Going Filipino is deliberate. Especially when I was in the US and Europe and I realized what was to be different in my dances. I did *Igorot* because it was also the most comfortable subject matter since I already wrote about it in a research paper and created a dance about it in my early years in my mother's studio."

After doing *Igorot,* which received critical acclaim locally and internationally, all other of Agnes' neo-ethnic[23] creations followed suit. *Bagobo* (1990), an all-female dance about Bagobo warriors and their ritual of human sacrifice, was Agnes' next neo-ethnic creation. Agnes did it after observing a Bagobo community called Sibunan. "Some of my friends said the work was feminist. I'm amazed. It's a simple human sacrifice in dance. You can read a lot of things in dance."

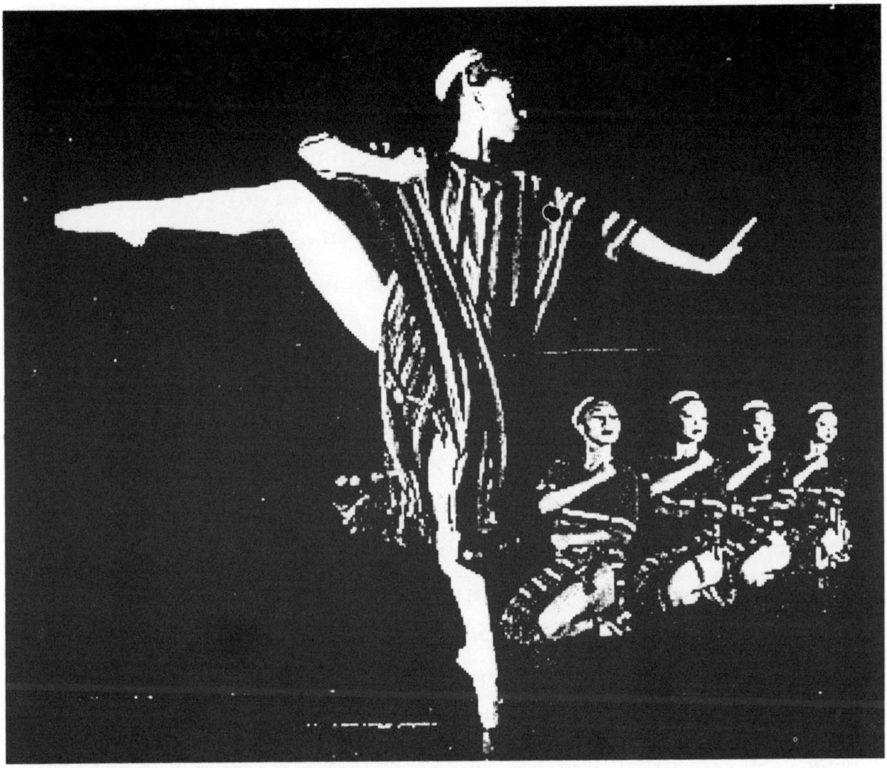

Taken from the priestess' pose in *Igorot,* Agnes' neo-ethnic ballet that garnered local and international critical acclaim.

Known for her "neoethnic" repertoire—a coinage of musician and her frequent collaborator Joey Ayala—Agnes also has to her credit a number of ethnic-inspired modern dances including *Muslim* (1990), *Moriones* (1991), *Hinilawod* (1991), and *Encantada* (1992). However, *Igorot* stands out because of its deliberate use of classical pointework of the ballet tradition, which she has not employed in the any of her other more earth-bound and non-balletic contemporary works.

As choreographer, Agnes situates herself within the frame of the past decade's trending of a "Philippine modern dance." It is inclined to what she calls "Philippine Movement Transformation [that is] consonant with the Filipinos' search for a national identity." While the 60s and 70s had ballets and modern dances influenced by Philippine folk dance, the late 80s up to the present saw a wealth of ethnic-inspired dances (Locsin 1999, 57). We can see here a parallel flourishing of indigenous forms and motifs in the 80s in visual arts, notably in Mindanao, as well as ethnic-inspired music in the vein of Joey Ayala's Bagong Lumad, Grace Nono, Ang Grupong Pendong, among others.

Philippine dance history mainly credits Leonor Orosa-Goquingco for pioneering folkloric or ethnic "Filipinized" ballets—such as the full-length *Filipinescas: Philippine Life, Legend and Lore* (1961) and her subsequent forays into return-to-native themes performed by her Filipinescas Dance Company (Villaruz 1999, 46)—which mainly offer romantic and idealized representations of a perceived Filipino native culture within the frame of a narrative and drama from Philippine legend, history, or literary sources[24] (CCP Encyclopedia 1994, 71). Ramon Obusan's Folkloric Dance Company staged in Manila, circa 1968 and 1974, a whole stylized program called *Kayaw* based on his research of Kalinga-Apayao dances. A host of other choreographers followed suit in this ethnic-folkloric vein: Julie Borromeo in *Kalingan* and Felicitas Radaic in *Nan-Pangkat* for Dance Theater Philippines; and Al Quinn and Corazon Inigo in *Lam-ang*, and Gener Caringal in *Tomaneg and Aniway*, both for the CCP Dance Company (Alejandro 1978, 143).

Agnes' roots in the land of the Mindanao *lumad*, influenced by fellow artist Joey Ayala—Davaoeño musician and lead of alternative performing group Bagong Lumad—provided the climate of inspiration to produce ethnic-influenced creations.

Dance research

Part of the choreographic process for Agnes is doing research. She is cautious of how she transposes indigenous styles into the idiom of modern dance stage performance.

"It takes, off and on, about a year to prepare for a major choreography. If I have to go to the mountains to do my research I don't hesitate to do it. I don't want to rely on other people's research works or depend on video tape recordings of tribal dances. I want to feel and experience the dance myself."

She has written at least three research papers about three different choreographic works which were read in various dance conferences. In her research paper "Transformation of the Aborignal Movement into Contemporary Choreography"[25]—for which she went to Surigao del Sur, Iloilo, Zambales, and Palawan for fieldwork—she discussed the research process of doing a solo called *Aeta,* and also related her views on her whole choreographic process.

> The choreographer has evolved a system of immersion that may well prove ineffective for the scholarly researcher but which serves my purpose. My main concern is to get the actual feel of the environment. Observation of daily activities becomes a necessity. The viewing of native dances is important only for reference. I depend on my eyes and other senses to absorb what goes on around me. Then I let my imagination roam. (Locsin 1998, 57)

In this paper, she first gave a brief history of dance in the Philippines, from tribal traditions to contemporary forms and movements. She locates herself within the period of the late 1980s to the present, which showed "an increase in the ethnic-inspired contemporary dances ... signaling an era of traditions and transformations." Further on, she defines her choreographic perspectives:

> *Choreography is creative work backed by research and artistic intuition,* the latter borne out of experience. Nuggets of information are gathered and interpreted into movement to achieve a contemporary look. *Exaggerated stylization is sometimes employed to distinguish the contemporary choreography from the authentic form.* (Ibid; italics mine)

Although her *Igorot* has received both rave reviews and critical assessments, Agnes consciously places her neo-ethnic works within the contemporary or modern dance idiom, not presenting them as a simplistic copy or replacement of the original Igorot dance traditions, nor the "authentic form" of the ethnic dances. For her, the ethnic and modern dances share strong affinities because of their earthiness and culturally grounded aesthetic. Thus, she allows her creativity to explore movement possibilities shared by the two forms of dancing.

Also, we can read how the balletic idiom in *Igorot* is radically ruptured and re-appropriated to serve as a form of representation of Cordillera culture. Dance critic Sally Ann Ness articulates:

> The message is emancipatory .... Whereas the Igorot vocabulary is given consistent stylistic and choreographic priority throughout the ballet, the movements of *classical ballet became an exploitable technology. The classical ballet vocabulary is re-adjusted, modified, and 'acculturated' so as to support a Philippine cultural agenda.* It is this manner that ballet becomes "Filipinized" in *Igorot*. (Ness 1997, 76; italics mine)

While ballet is manipulated towards such ends, we should inquire, however, about what exactly constitutes a generalized "Philippine cultural agenda." The notion of "Filipinizing" art is not completely unproblematic with tendencies of nativist sentiments and exoticizing non-Western cultures. It is still the role of dance critics to interrogate, and not just rave about, the constructed notions that dances bear and inscribe in their productions.

Christine Maranan, one of the dancers of *Igorot*, says that they "want to bring their culture onstage through a different medium in another form of dance." This acknowledgment of using a "different medium" and "another form of dance" is a dancer's informed recognition of the "different," because colonial, dance form of ballet, as opposed to the tradition of the Igorot peoples, and thus also a recognition of the multiple construction of their bodies required by this neoethnic choreographic project. Her statement assumes that there is no necessary privileging of this "different medium"—the theater-performed ballet—over the dance culture of the Cordillera peoples.

Agnes is aware of some critics saying that *Igorot* is "exoticizing" Igorot culture. She is not bothered, however, because she backs her works with field research, grounded in her role as a choreographer paying tribute to a cultural tradition through the modern ballet idiom. It is in this frame of definition that we can read Agnes' attempt at neoethnic choreography as a cultural homage, in theatrical form, to indigenous dance cultures this country is heir to.

> *Neo-ethnic works pay tribute to tradition, and in no way attempt to replace or erase it.* To do so, the choreographer must take pains to retain the essence or soul of the dance despite the modernization of the movements. (Locsin 1999, 57; italics mine)

It is in maintaining this artistic autonomy of creating and re-inventing new ways of presenting *othered* and marginalized ethnic cultures in her own artistic vocabulary that has, in a sense, become Agnes' cause, given her exposure to the plight of the *lumads* in Mindanao. Though not inclined to take up advocacies and causes, Agnes remains a consummate technician exploring dance cultures and forms in her own responsible way as a creative artist.

She further asserts her aim, completely of a different track from earlier efforts at dance research such as Francisca Reyes-Tolentino's (later Aquino) pioneering research on Philippine folk dance:

> Mrs. Francisca Reyes depicted tribal and folk dance per se, meaning whatever she saw, she taught exactly. *I create new movements. I just get inspiration from the tribal dances that I see or research on. As far as I know, I have my original steps.* I know for a fact that I created the steps and did not lift them from anywhere else. But of course you cannot claim originality on anything because it is not strange for somebody to come up with probably similar steps from another place. That happens, but the compositions, the putting together, the embellishing of the movements are all mine. I have an independent style of my own.[26] (Italics mine)

Though she claims to mostly work based on "gut-feel" and "instinct" like her mother does, she decided several years ago to write down her choreographic process into several points to serve as tips for younger choreographers. She came up with the following preliminary ideas: *concept, research and immersion, music, movement theme, design (set and costume), structure and substructure, transitions, special problems, ending, and critiquing.* She has yet to elaborate in written form the finer aspects of these concepts.

Finally, it is Agnes' multi-layered identity as a contemporary Filipino "mestiza" that enables her to speak in different cultural registers. As Sally Ann Ness would locate where Agnes belongs within the various postcolonial predicaments of transnational and cross-cultural desires and identities:

> The non-Oriental aspects of the choreography speak to Locsin's own *mestiza* postcolonial cultural predicament .... Locsin 'speaks' essentially in the classical European vocabulary of ballet, but she incorporates as well choreographic statements originated in 'non-Western' Philippine dance practices. *Igorot* does not deny but rather maintains continuity between generations of artists in the Philippines, managing in the process to construct within its aesthetic domain a Filipino-hood that is something more than a tactic of transnational politics or economics, and something more than the strategy of a developing country's agenda for nation-building. Igorot constructs bodies that did not originate simply in the moment of Philippine independence, nor only at the site of the CCP, nor in the ballet studios of Europe or North America or Manila, nor, most certainly, in the Cordilleran highlands. *Its bodies have originated within complex cultural, individual, and social histories.* (Ness 1997, 68; italics mine)

Agnes' other future neoethnic works received less controversy; after *Igorot,* she used the contemporary idiom of barefooted dancing instead of the balletic pointe work that became such a contentious yet enriching site of cultural discourse among local and international critics.[27]

Dance as education and empowerment

Although she uses mostly women dancers even for male roles—as in *Igorot* where warrior and priest roles were danced by women, and in

Bagobo where the warriors were also all-female dancers—Agnes does not claim any affinity to feminism as an inspiration for her creation of dances. She says it was mainly because of the lack of male dancers at that time she created them, hinting too that it was women dancers who have trained more proficiently in the field. Although many of the dance narratives she choreographed have used strong female characters, including *Babaylan* (1992), *Encantada* (1992), and *Salome* (1998), Agnes says she treats men and women as equals when she works with them. She surmises that perhaps it is because she has never herself experienced prejudice as a woman in the dance world and has always felt empowered by her dancing and dance-making.

"Dance has been a source of empowerment and education," Agnes says. "I've learnt so much and seen many places because of dance, and it has enriched me as a person." She is aware, however, that dance for women can be especially competitive and that dancers in general are "gypsies" open to exploitable conditions. She still gets in touch with some of the dancers she has trained in BP who have gone to different places to dance; some are under vulnerable conditions because of the lack of funding given to dance, here and elsewhere. They would time and again continue to communicate with her—as students would with a respected teacher—for advice.

New and recent works

One of Agnes' recent independent productions is *Sayaw Likhang Kiukok* (2003), inspired by the works of fellow Davaoeño National Artist for Visual Arts Ang Kiukok. In this, she further stretched the earlier thirty-second work she did for Kiukok, which was one of the works commissioned by the CCP in 2001 as a tribute to the 11 National Artists in the visual arts. In this work, she has used angular, jagged, almost mannequin-like movements by barefoot dancers to show the cubist angst of Kiukok's works, which mostly center on decrepit urban life. Dancers Gaye Galiluyo, Gerald Mercado, and Jill Raya were the main dancers of the performance. The show was given a grant by the National Commission for Culture and the Arts (NCCA) as part of its February Arts Month program.

In 2000, she set-up *Dance and Poetry*, where she interpreted in movements the works of Davao poets Tita Lacambra Ayala, Jo Bacani Angeles, Alfrredo Salanga, and Ricardo de Ungria. A similarly themed show is *Sayaw Atbp.* (2001), where she showcased dances inspired by literary and visual art works of Aida Rivera Ford, Jose Ayala, Bert Monterona, and Ricardo de Ungria, among others. More and more, we see here the collaborative and cross-disciplinal nature of Agnes' works as she draws from literature and the visual arts. Her regular audience is mainly composed of artists, young professionals, students and teachers, and of course, contacts and friends of the school's own dance students.

On the side, Agnes has also taken choreographic projects for Lisa Macuja-Elizalde's Ballet Manila, for which she has done *Agila* (2003) and *Ritwal* (2003), two neoethnic solos that were part of the dance company's entries for dance competitions in Tokyo and New York. Besides this, Agnes is also regularly invited to do theater choreographies, such as for Tanghalang Pilipino's *Ang Pagpatay kay Antonio Luna* (2002) and *Hudhud* (2004), PETA's *Operang Tatlumpera* (1998), and SK Entertainment's *Rama at Sita* (1999). She used to take choreographies for high-paying commercial companies—*"raket"* in Filipino colloquy—but has now decided to focus more on developing and evolving new works in her own studio.

She believes that it would take ten years for dancers to become proficient in a choreographer's vocabulary. So far, she has had three years of teaching a younger set of dancers in their studio and looks forward to the coming years.

Motherly instincts

Agnes has earned several awards for her choreographies. She won second place in the Prince Takamado Award at the 1992 Tokyo International Choreographic Competition for her *Moriones,* and won the same award in 1993 for *Babaylan. Salome,* a solo from a larger dance *Elias* based on the Rizal novel, garnered the silver medal for dancer Camille Ordinario in the 1992 Paris International Dance Competition. Her *Taong Talangka* also got the silver medal in the 1994 Paris Modern Dance Competition. Locally, she has been awarded the Datu Bago Award from the City of Davao (2000) for her prolific work as a Davao-based artist.

Amidst the prestige of being a multi-awarded choreographer, what she prizes most are her students whom the considers to be her jewels. Agnes has remained single all these years and considers her students to be her own children.

"They're my babies," Agnes relates with affection. "I have worked with many dancers and helped them grow and perform to the maximum of their abilities. Being with my dancers, I experience the closest that a mother could feel. When I see them dance with their souls, my heart swells with pride." She says that her "pride and joy" is her nephew, Sonny Locsin, whom she trained as a ballet dancer in their family studio, until he went to dance with BP; he is now dancing professionally in Europe. Others who have been part of the BP II such as Paul Morales (now of Airdance) occasionally get in touch with her for advice. She also invites former BP dancers like Christine Maranan, Gaye Galiluyo, and Gerald Mercado to be part of her more recent independent productions in Davao.

Agnes, now home-bound, sees many benefits in working on her own, independent of the institutions she has served for most of her professional career:

> I'm less tense and I feel like I'm my own person. In the institution, you are hounded by work, deadline, pressure, politics, and more endless work. On my own I get to do things at my own pace. You don't have to kill yourself to do something you like. I can still come up with good dances and make people happy. I take care of the costume and lighting. My cousin is an artist who does some of the stage design. I have very minimal expenses too. I just go to Aldevinco (a local store) to get my dancers dressed.

She says that none of the dancers she has worked with has ever asked for money from her when they dance in her productions, observing that it has been that sheer love and fun of learning dance together that brought them to take classes and dance for her classes and shows. However, recognizing their hard work, she maintains her financial commitment of paying her dancers when they perform in her productions, whether they are Davao- or Manila-based. "*Wala pa namang* dancer *na naningil sa akin* because they look at me as a teacher. But I pay them anyway. We have a very symbiotic relationship—we learn and take from each other."

She also has found more time to do other things besides teach and create dance, like gardening, farming, looking after her dogs, and just being company to her mother.

"Sometimes I dread choreographing, *baka walang lumabas*. It's an aim to constantly evolve. So I enjoy my non-teaching time. I'm here now in our school to make good products, follow my mother's footsteps and stretch it even further. But I'm thankful that I don't have to choreograph like I used to when I was bound to an institution. There's more space to breathe," Agnes beams, pleased that she has now—as in her pre-CCP years—regained her self-defined space of creativity as an independent dance artist.

Notes

1. All quotes in this section were taken from an interview with Myra Beltran dated March 14, 2000, unless otherwise indicated.

2. Also refer to a larger paper I wrote on this dance titled "Dancing and other Necessities: Women Seizing Spaces for an Empowering Dance Aesthetic" in *Philippine Humanities Review*. Forthcoming.

3. Joanne was Myra's batchmate and best friend in BP and is now a full-time mother while Christine is from a younger generation of BP dancers who also left the company to strike it on her own in dance.

4. *Fragile Circle* and *Daughters of Necessity* were both partially sponsored by the National Commission for Culture and the Arts. The NCCA granted her the Gawad Alab ng Haraya Award in year 2000 for Individual Recognition in Performing Art.

5. See a more detailed discussion I wrote on Myra's alternative dance space titled "Space, Body, Woman: Dance-Making and Space-Claiming at a Studio Theater in 38 West Avenue" in *Bulawan Journal for Philippine Arts and Culture*, Issue 10.

6. From conversations with Myra Beltran, June 6, 2004.

7. Now a multi-awarded US-based independent dancer, Labayen came back from San Francisco last year to stage a show with her entitled *Damas Confuria at the Beltran studio-theater.*

8. Myra only started a year ago the project of recording personal thoughts on her dances. So far, she has written only this lone entry on her first production, and intends to do the same with her other succeeding works.

9. All quotes in this section were taken from an interview with Kristin Jackson dated January 20 and February 11, 2003, unless otherwise indicated.

10. From an e-mail correspondence with Kristin Jackson dated March 22, 2004.

11. Kristin further elaborates her difference with Merce Cunningham's chance method in another correspondence dated June 11, 2004. She shares:

"Merce Cunningham does use the 'chance' method but his process is a little different from mine. Cunningham usually has set movement phrases that he and his dancers put together in non-linear ways. For example, dice is thrown to determine the order of the movement. His dancers then are challenged to create 'transitions' in order to connect these disparate sections of movement—but always informed by Cunningham's vision and aesthetic, of course."

12. Kristin also elaborates on Ruth Currier in the following terms: "Ruth Currier was teaching a choreography workshop at a dance studio in NY the summer before I entered NYU. It was the first choreography class I had ever taken. I used the work that I developed in her class (a preliminary study for "Field") to audition for the graduate program at Tisch." From an email correspondence dated June 11, 2004.

13. From an e-mail correspondence with Kristin Jackson dated March 22, 2004.

14. Taken from the choreographer's notes of Kristin Jackson in *Threshold*, Cultural Center of the Philippines, 1993.

15. E-mail correspondence with Kristin Jackson dated June 2, 2003.

16. Ibid.

17. This is particularly true in Ballet Philippines where classes and rehearsals would stretch from 2 pm to 10 pm. From my personal experience of dance rehearsals in another ballet school/company, these can also reach up to very late at night and can depend on the erratic whims of the artistic director/choreographer.

18. This unpublished critical paper for the course "Philippine Art: Sources and Influences"is titled "Transgressing Cultures: Reading the Neoethnic of Agnes Locsin's Igorot."

19. All quotes in this section were taken from an interview with Agnes Locsin dated January 5-9, 2004, unless otherwise indicated.

20. Agnes was director of her high school dance group, Terpsichoreans.

21. Quote from "The Irrepresible Agnes Locsin" by Michael Ebro Dakudao, *Sunstar Davao*, April 2, 2000. pp W1–W2.

22. Even before Agnes came in as CCP faculty, modern dance was previously taught in the company mainly by Alice Reyes, Luis Layag, Basilio Esteban Villaruz, Tony Fabella, and other visiting teachers.

23. Before the onslaught of dances in the Ballet Philippines repertoire dubbed "neo-ethnic," Denisa Reyes already enunciated the term "neo-Filipino" to refer to Filipino modern ballets. Neo-ethnic works came later which specifically showed themes from Philippine indigenous dance movements.

24. This is shown in *Trend: Return to Native, Filipinescas: Philippine Life, Legend and Lore,* and the *Noli Dance Suite.*

25. This research was funded by a research grant under the Toyota Foundation.

26. Quote from "The Irrepresible Agnes Locsin" by Michael Ebro Dakudao, *Sunstar Davao,* April 2, 2000. pp W1–W2.

27. Read Sally Ann Ness' "Originality in the Postcolony" for a more detailed discussion of various local and international perspectives that the dance has stirred. See my bibliography for reference details.

CHAPTER 5

An Aesthetic of Independence

While the aesthetic of independence resists fixture as a stable and unitary practice, it remains clear that "independent dance-making" as practiced by the three women dance-makers is firmly grounded in their specific locations and subjections. This makes their aesthetic self-reflexive and relevant to their contexts as women creating and sharing their art.

Let us surface the multiplicity of their strengths in their modes of practicing independence in dance, and note some critical tendencies in their dance practice that we can inspect and reflect on.

Re-grounding the body. Myra's regrounding of ballet convention to her bodily experience as a contemporary Filipina deconstructs the body of the female ballerina that is homogenized by the Western ideal of feminine beauty in the classical ballet aesthetic. Her self-defined practice of remaining grounded in ballet steps and yet freely improvising them is part of her subversive mode of dancing, independent of the hegemonic traditions of ballet schools and companies where she has previously trained and worked with. The myth of the ideal classical ballerina—characterized by her pleasing lightness and docile interpretation of ballet technique—is shattered with Myra's critique of the tenets of the romantic ballet traditions that feminize and idealize the female dancer as a passive and submissive body who performs for the pleasure of a male-defined gaze. Myra exhibits in her dances the displeasing and unpleasant images of a woman perennially caught up in a world of emotional dissonance, inner discontentment, interpreting the interior contours of feeling and sentiment associated with her struggles as a woman in a tradition-bound dance world.

However, one tendency exemplified in these attempts is the constant romanticization of the self in constant struggle, angst, and despair, forever ensnared in a web of sorrow—mainly signified by the facial demeanor that she expresses in most, if not all, of her works. Such consistent allusion to woman in the habitual mood and attitude of despair may only reinforce the figure of woman-as-victim, a disempowering stereotype in the patriarchal imagery of woman. So far, I can recall only two of her dances which seem to have broken this trademark mold of anguish and desolation, specifically *Daughters of Necessity* which is a forward-looking piece of hope and solidarity for women, and *Sisters,* a light piece about the comforting and playful company of sisterhood. Perhaps by exploring a range of other self-empowering emotions and ideas in her dances—such as in her most recent work *Confuria* which shows affirmative female strength through its subversive mockery of religious traditions—Myra could evolve further her repertoire of choreographies that offer more positive and empowering images of women.

Although Myra used to think of herself as the lone independent woman dancer in the country, coming from a purist conception of independent dancing as a "solitary movement" of one person, she has now pioneered notable collaborative efforts with younger independent dance groups, particularly with the aforementioned Contemporary Dance Map in years 2005 and 2006, as well as the "Wi Fi Body Independent Dance Festival" in 2006. In these collaborative efforts, she seems to have recovered from the propensity to romanticize her own space and place as one of solitude, sadness, and marginality to one of sharing, collegiality, and community with kindred dance professionals.

Sharing of self. Kristin comes from a rich cross-cultural experience of Filipino diaspora in America, within which she thrived with a self-defined minimalist dance style, and a pedagogy of egalitarian dance practice and collaborative sharing of self—whether in the dance studio as a dance-maker, or in the university classroom as a college teacher.

Despite Kristin's meaningful explorations of the nuances of her multicultural heritage, she still construes dance as a "universal language"—a problematic idea in its tendency to universalize and totalize a conception of dance that can reach audiences beyond boundaries of race, class, and gender. But with her admission of the "special role" of women in the dance world in the way that they "humanize" the art form, Kristin remains grounded in her specific role and subjectivity as a woman in dance. As an independent dancer and choreographer, collaborating with and nurturing dancers as her peers, we see Kristin's strength as a dance educator. She genuinely lives and develops an alternative pedagogy of egalitarian relationships among the different agents in the art and dance world who take part in her creative process of dance-making—quietly countering the prevalent iniquitous transactions surrounding the hierarchical master-apprentice system in the dance world.

Returning home. Agnes, in her recent return to her provincial roots in Davao City, brings us back to the place that nurtured her dancing and prepared her for the discipline and rigor of independent dance practice and production. We saw how her home-grown and locally rooted dance training in the land of the Mindanao *lumad* (ethnic) would strongly influence her making of neoethnic choreographies even after her masteral dance training in the US, until she embarked into the CCP's Ballet Philippines, first as faculty, and later as its chief choreographer and artistic director.

Among the three dance artists in this study, Agnes is considered to be the most institutional and mainstream because she has been closely associated with major urban cultural agencies such as the CCP and BP for most of her professional career. Very few people know her independent beginnings as a young dancer and choreographer in Davao, and her choice to return to the place of her early thriving years where she resumed the practice of independently creating dances and teaching local dancers in her mother's sixty-year-old dance school.

Although still rooted in the traditional master-apprentice system of teaching ballet and modern movements, Agnes is currently experimenting with more contemporary and collaborative approaches to dance. This is seen in her collaborative works in her Davao studio, where she feels more keen to experiment and evolve as a dance-maker, what with her freer time sans the pressure of deadlines and company politics.

As an independent dance-maker, Agnes openly takes on choreographic projects for dance companies and theater groups—as part of her maintaining close relationships with other cultural workers in the field—and sometimes, for commercial companies, to serve as her bread-and-butter. Her honesty and openness to acknowledge her fellow collaborators in the art and dance world makes her idea and definition of independent dancing a practical and lived one, something that she is not inclined to romanticize or exclusively brandish only for herself. Being an independent dance artist for her is simply a choice that was borne out of necessity stemming from both personal creativity and economic need.

As an ardent and seasoned technician of movements, Agnes creates dances that audiences can watch with similar wonder and interest, as seen in *Igorot* and her other neoethnic works that tend to astound and interest audiences with their masterful artistry of dance styles and techniques. She is more inclined toward the exterior configurations of combining dance forms rather than going into the depths of cultural issues, its various representations, struggles and contradictions. Although grounded in field and archival research, Agnes has been cautioned by audiences and critics against the perils of exoticizing indigenous cultures in her neoethnic works. Furthermore, unlike Myra and Kristin who delve into dances with themes about the inner self and that can be executed by only one to five dancers in small spaces, Agnes has mainly composed grand dance dramas and narratives with expansive movements and huge casts that are ideally set up for big theaters, such as *Encantada, Elias,* and *La Revolucion Filipina*. However, her other works like *Bagobo, Dabaw, Salome,* and *Sayaw Likhang Kiukok* powerfully show her delving into the inner landscape and issues of the self and its larger social milieu. With the fresh atmosphere of her home, Agnes, now low-key and privately confined, still evolves new ways of dance-making.

Dancing from Elsewhere: Independence as Difference

The narratives of the three dance-makers are replete with signs and signals of their dancing from elsewhere:* away from the spaces that they have called home, and in reclamation of their own self-defined spaces. This elsewhere is a space both of difference and dislocation, a space where they were able to define and experience being independent from the traditional and the mainstream of dance practice and culture.

Notice that all three women share an experience of moving and migrating from home to exile, from center to periphery, from mainstream to margins. This physical relocation has also become psychic and aesthetic. It heightened their experiences of being "othered" as cultural exiles or outsiders—experiences from which they gained invaluable perspectives and insights about dancing and living in another place, while maintaining a sense of integrity and independence as women and as dance artists.

Myra's sense of deterritorialization as a dancer in institutional ballet companies in Germany and Yugoslavia has served as a turning point for her to realize her cultural difference as a Filipina. Even as she came back home to dance professionally with Ballet Philippines, that sense of displacement and alienation from the traditions of the classical ballet aesthetic still pervaded and has led her to question and aspire for another

* I use this idea of "elsewhere" in this writing to define the alternative space of independence and difference that women dance-makers in this study have mobilized and occupied to assert their autonomous aesthetic in dancing. Griselda Pollock, borrowing from Teresa De Lauretis's conception of a feminist elsewhere, the space-off or blind spots of hegemonic discourses within the masculine canon, offers a decidedly feminist recuperation of Edouard Manet's canonical painting "A Bar at the Folies-Bergere." De Lauretis defines this elsewhere as "the margins of hegemonic discourses, social spaces carved in the interstices of institutions and in the chinks and cracks of the power-knowledge apparati." (Lauretis in Pollock 1996b, 280)

place and space that could contain her *othered* sense of culture and aesthetic in dance.

Kristin's emigration to the US served to strengthen her aesthetic of independence in the dance world. In New York, she found the proper atmosphere that nurtured and refined her own search for a different movement style amidst the diverse and competing modern and contemporary dance movements in the US. Her identity as Filipino-American-Irish has further sensitized and informed her works which tend to draw from her various trans-cultural experiences as an Asian amidst the flux of diasporic cultures overseas. Her idea of independence and difference is also marked by the humaneness she imbues into relationships with her fellow dancers—indeed a different mode of relating amidst the pervasive and abusive hierarchies in traditional dance company structures.

In Agnes' case, her articulation of difference arose from her experience of being a Davaoeña in Manila who made it to the institutional canon of modern choreographers through sheer determination and hard work. As a dance-maker, she was differently grounded in the way that she firmly took inspiration from her ethnic and cultural roots in the lumad land of Mindanao. Her theatrical mind and technical skills in ballet and modern dance traditions, honed in their independently run dance school and briefly developed through graduate studies in the US, influenced Agnes to appropriate indigenous themes and motifs into her choreographic works for a major institutional dance company, mainly as part of the dance company's ethic of choreographic innovation and its projection of national identity. Once the *probinsyana* in Manila, Agnes is now decidedly home in Davao, on her own as a seasoned and independent dance practitioner, beginning anew in the project of making dances and teaching dancers in her mother's home-grown, independently-run school.

It is in their assertion of their marked political and aesthetic difference, coupled with their determined and persevering work ethic, that the three dance-makers have inhabited and straddled various worlds and spaces, and moved closer to a self-defined elsewhere that is their own independent dance practice. They have chosen to reclaim and reoccupy an elsewhere that is at once physical and psychic. Their shift from center to margins is a crucial act of moving towards independence, a gesture thriving with notions of artistic responsibility, self-empowered creativity, and autonomous dance-making. Indeed, they have claimed for themselves an aesthetic of difference from the mainstream and the dominant in contemporary Philippine dance practice.

CHAPTER 6

Performing Genealogies

In reading the stories of three independent women dance-makers, we have witnessed the diverse strands of going independent in the contemporary Philippine dance world. A common thread weaving through their histories is the moment of claiming personal space and autonomy, away from the major institutional agencies that they were once part of. Maturing through time in their professions, we see them aspiring for greater room in exercising their personal freedom and artistic dignity to produce other ways of practicing, teaching, and creating dances.

While all three first developed within the classical ballet tradition which provided their formative dance training, they each later developed different idioms in their explorations into modern and contemporary dance. Each artist also has her own unique and distinct way of practicing and producing herself in the dance world. Some, like Myra, have claimed the term more assertively than the others, but this does not diminish the possibility of the term being used and practiced by others who are less conscious of it but have also practically appropriated its radical possibilities.

All three have grown at different times, milieu, and circumstances in Philippine dance and therefore have developed different articulations of their practice as dancers, choreographers, or dance teachers. One common ground is that they are all middle class, well-educated, and trained in and exposed to dance abroad. That they have remained free from the responsibilities of motherhood as childless (Kristin) or single women (Myra and Agnes) was also a factor that allowed them greater personal and psychic freedom to explore more novel paths into their dance careers.

Narrating their personal histories as dancers and dance-makers foregrounds their multiple subjectivities as women, daughters, cultural workers, teachers, family members, advocates, and thinkers in their own right. This leads us to another common theme found in their stories: the sense of self-empowerment dancing offered them as they experienced and practiced the profession.

Dissatisfied with the way dancers' voices were muted and unrecognized in the major dance companies she had worked with, and inspired by the relative freedom of independent dance groups in Europe, Myra consciously trail-blazed the path of independent dance practice when she returned to the country, with the motivation from a local mentor and other artists she has collaborated with in the field. This has set her to explore her own psychic and aesthetic space as a woman dancer, and claim her own vocabulary of dancing in a literally small and marginal dance space. Kristin has gathered many experiences of dancing in her own country, that—after deciding to make it in the US as a dancer—would eventually lead her to teach dance to college students while defining her own independent dance aesthetic as choreographer and director of Kristin Jackson Dance. Meanwhile, Agnes' trajectory as a seasoned choreographer was disposed by the independently run dance studio of her mother in Davao City, and later, by her graduate dance studies in the US. She would later move to a major Manila-based dance institution, rising from the ranks, from being faculty to artistic director and resident choreographer. Eventually she chose to return to her regional roots, independently creating and teaching dance in her mother's dance school.

Although all three of them have broken away from the dance company system at various periods in their artistic lives, they still continue to link up in collaborative works with various dance and cultural groups or institutions—both large and small scale—and take on teaching stints or freelance choreographic projects for various theater and dance companies from time to time.

It is in this sense that independent dance is not one fixed and definitive practice, but one that is appropriated by dance artists to refer to their various expressions of artistic autonomy and personal freedom in their similar yet varied ways of practicing and defining dance.

Prospects and Possibilities of Independent Dance in Contemporary Philippines

I found that there are different degrees or levels of being an independent artist, and that there is a sense of fluidity in working inside and outside the institutional dance world. The term "independent" is therefore not a rigid construction but a contestable site of negotiation for the three women under study. Thus, going independent could mean any one or a combination of these possibilities: a) creating an alternative dance space away from the major institutional theater/dance spaces, b) breaking away from dance company membership and practice, c) establishing and creating one's own dance productions, d) self-financing dance practices and productions or practicing non-traditional dance aesthetics (i.e. non-ballet, usually modern or contemporary dance).

As validated by the abovementioned findings, the idea of being an "independent dance artist" is still an inchoate term as it is a relatively recent phenomenon and object of study in Philippine dance scholarship. The dancers' breaking-away from the institutional ballet school tradition and institutional funding, does not prevent them from getting their audience, circle of dancers, and even grants and funding from the mainstream institutions such as the NCCA, CCP, and Fulbright. Being independent therefore is not a fixed but a shifting term and practice.

Myra Beltran, for instance, consciously established herself as a self-defined independent dancer, in terms of having her own private non-traditional dance space and aesthetics of dance practice, at the same time producing her own dances as artistic director of Dance Forum. She has, however, sourced funding within the auspices of the NCCA and has collaborated with dancers from Philippine Ballet Theater, UP Dance Company, and Ballet Philippines. Agnes Locsin, on the other hand, while having worked in a dominant cultural institution as artistic director of Ballet Philippines, is foremost a home-grown dancer from Davao under the tutelage of her mother's local ballet school such that even as she was with CCP/BP, she already felt that she was independently exploring her own dance idiom (through neoethnic ballet). Having resigned from BP, she returned to her Davao roots, in her own mother's dance school, teaching young dancers the craft, and putting up her own shows and new choreographies. She calls herself an independent artist in this sense, as she feels greater freedom to work at her own pace and is not tied to dance company politics, and has more time to do projects with theater people, dance groups, and other freelance dancers in Manila and Davao. For her part, Kristin Jackson finds it "easier" to be a practicing independent dance artist in America as there is more funding and economic support available, despite the fact that there is also greater competition for space and funding among the many currently emerging independent artists in the US. While teaching dance in the academe, she also has found the freedom to be able to create her own dances with a set of independent dancers she constantly works and collaborates with.

All these experiences show the articulations of going "independent" in terms of personal history, economy, politics, and personal aesthetics in dance.

It should be noted that it is *women* from the *middle and upper classes* who have more access to ballet and the dance system in general. This is because, 1) of their possession of economic and symbolic means to physically and culturally appropriate dance, and 2) of their being *women*—dance being a "feminine and female" endeavor. In contrast to women, men in dance—as dance scholar Basilio Esteban Villaruz points out—usually come from economically disadvantaged classes, and face familial and social backlash in being stereotyped as gays for entering a feminized field. In the Philippine setting, this is seen in the apparent hegemony of women in the dance world: it is largely led by female artistic directors (refer to *Chapter III-Generations and Genealogies: Women in Philippine Ballet and Modern Dance*), and receives patronage from upper-class women such as the likes of former First Ladies Imelda Marcos and Amelita Ramos, National Artist Lucresia Kasilag, writer Beth Day Romulo, media magnates Emily Abrera and Maan Hontiveros, to mention but a few.

One constraint of going independent, especially in a Third World country such as the Philippines, is the expensive requirement of setting-up and maintaining regular independent dance shows, which necessitates rehearsing and choreographing dancers, finding regular performance spaces, having adequate funding, and mobilizing a considerably consistent audience support. Myra and Agnes are particularly advantaged in the aspect of performance space since they have permanent performance venues conveniently found within their own family property. Kristin meanwhile benefits from the availability of funding resources and venue grants for enterprising American-Asian artists like her, especially in an economically-privileged location that is New York City.

Furthermore, all three artists have their previous affiliation with dance institutions to back them up and make them credible to award- and grant-giving institutions such as the NCCA, CCP, and Fulbright. Given the lack of funding that is locally given and made available to the arts, independent dance practice will most likely remain expensive, inaccessible, if not wholly unknown to the less advantaged quarters in Philippine society. This should inexorably be the case unless independent dancers grow into a critical and conscientious mass and establish a support system for their endeavors and projects like that of the Independent Artists Network in the United Kingdom.

The fledgling though sustained endeavors of the World Dance Alliance Philippines in the years 2005 to 2006 to hold pioneering contemporary dance festivals for independent groups are a most welcome and refreshing enterprise from a younger generation of emerging independent dancers and groups.

Women Rethinking Dance: Summary of Challenges Encountered in Present Paths

One of the main challenges I encountered in this research was that of searching for archival materials about independent dancers, given the virtual inexistence of a systematic body of literature regarding this. Thus, we confront the task of defining independent dance practice, and at the same time underlining the gendered agency of women dancing independently. There is also a challenge in terms of merging dance history as a disciplinal framework within the broader but distinct disciplinal frame of art history, which has largely dealt with visual arts and waylaid dance. This, however, is a possibility opened up by the new art histories, which are pluralized to represent the non-traditional narratives of multiple subjectivities and othered histories, and therefore challenge the traditional notion of one canonical construction that is usually a patriarchal and Euro-American-centered history of art.

The critical inflection "feminist" in these dance histories is also an additional but necessary and significant political category in the writing of the histories of these three independent women dance artists. New categories are set up, proposed, and explored by the researcher for this type of pioneering study in Philippine dance history and feminist studies in Philippine academia, categories mainly drawn from feminist thinkers and art/dance researchers, and given localized form in my grounding as a young Filipino woman straddling both the academic and dance worlds. This makes for a richer trans-disciplinal inquiry that draws from the emergent ideas within the disciplines of art history, dance history and criticism, and women's/feminist studies. One idea for a future gender-focused scholarly study of dance is one that tackles the plight and status of male dance-makers in the Philippine dance world*—whether in institutional or independent dance practice—as their particular subjectivities would register a different constellation of aesthetic, practice, and discourse in Philippine dance and culture.

* I am thankful to Prof. Steve Villaruz for intimating about the equally neglected and unstudied plight of male dancers/dance-makers in Philippine dance.

CHAPTER 7

Re-writing as Gesture from Elsewhere

In both word and gesture I have refigured here the stories of three independent women dance-makers. Positioned in a space that is both distant yet near, inside yet outside, I engage myself in the interventionist task of notating the stories of three women in dance, whose plot is unmistakably overlaid with prominent markings as well as concealed traces.

As I write their stories, I take on the identities of an art history scholar, a young woman dancer, and a contemporary feminist—subjectivities that make me slip through spaces, cross boundaries, and plot out new routes of defiance. This project rejects phallogocentric reasoning which construes anything bodily to be non-intellectual. I become the choreographer of this textual performance, doing both dancing and writing, gesturing while historicizing, setting into motion a discursive dialogue with the three women dance artists by interacting with their histories and restaging them in the performative moment of my own texts and contexts. Choreographing their histories, and historicizing their choreographies, I stage here a personal performance of defiance by invoking three other women's stories amidst our diverse yet shared corporealities of dancing, theorizing, and historicizing.

Independent dancer and researcher Carol Brown similarly suggests how she disrupts the Western androcentric logic of linearity and objectivity through her disciplinal and discursive negotiations as a dancing academic. By decentralizing traditional knowledge and exploring other registers of knowing and being known, she effectively upsets the patriarchal order of the bifurcation of body and mind, research subject and object, performer and spectator:

> Choreographing theory and theorizing choreography means constant interruptions; one type of activity substitutes another as I move from one kind of space to another through different registers of corporeality .... Inscribing theory through practice means exploring the materiality of ideas through the intermeshing of discourses. Dancing across the borders of diverse fields of knowledge and cultural spaces involves surprise and the unexpected. *Navigating these unexpected occurrences ruptures my own expectations, splintering the homogeneity of a singular point of view through new couplings between texts and movements, bodies and theories. Making a spectacle of theory in this way mutates disciplines, creating new hybrid forms which displace distinctions between critic and performer, theorist and practitioner, body and knowledge.* (1997, 136; italics mine)

And so this narrative has been a genealogical performance requiring from me its own requisite choreography of personal memory, collective history, and emergent discourse. Mobilizing the emergent politics of feminist dance histories in this very writing is a form of independent performance in the field of research and critical historical writing. This rewriting of stories is an undertaking leading to an emancipatory theory of a feminist aesthetic of women's independent dance practice in the Philippine dance field—indeed a move toward a feminist historiography of dance.

This attempt to retell the stories of three dance-mothers is also a personal process of re-learning what it means to dance and to perceive dance differently from what I was originally taught within tradition-bound ballet schools. And yet at the end of this re-telling, I find myself unapologetic for having remained singly trained in classical ballet all these years, coming as I am from a personal preference and bodily comfort in "dancing back" to what my body has been made familiar of. I remain a ballet dancer, convention-bound to a classical Western dance form, yet openly engaging in this dialogue with three women dance-makers who attempt to upstage this long-held dance tradition by their various modes of practicing independence in dance.

This makes this narrative of three women's bodies a story of my own dancing body as well. This act of retrieval and rewriting is a personal act, a cross-generational motion to gather lessons from an emergent and contemporary dance tradition that I have not yet dared to explore as a young woman dancing. This act of restaging their histories, this act of writing from an elsewhere, is an attempt at an engagement of their inheritance to us in the field of scholarly research and writing.

And so, this writing as a performance has become a significant personal repossession of a dance genealogy and legacy: this retelling commits to personal memory and collective history the artistic legacies of three seasoned and independent women dance-makers, whose stories would otherwise be left mis- or un-represented within the dominant narratives of traditional art and dance history. This act of rewriting a "history of the present" is what Michel Foucault calls a "critical genealogy," where history is not anymore about merely tracing roots and origins, but one of recovering displacements and dislocations in history and culture.

Dancer and researcher Leslie Satin argues that dance has been used by women as a persistent mode of telling personal tales, an autobiographical expression that enacts their selves and stories precisely because of the lack of open spaces for their re-telling:

> The history of women and autobiography is the history of women's lack of access to the public forum and the multiple ways in which women have sought after and fought for that access, either through private texts or open arenas (acts of non-textual rebellion, or the making public of texts) .... Nonetheless, feminist discomfort which has arisen about the meaning for women of the proverbial "death of the author" is particularly germane to female autobiography, when neither the life nor the author has full cultural significance. This instability is replicated in western concert dance, whose relatively recent history includes a progression of women of great power but also idealizes and romanticizes that power. These women and their work may be thought of as trespassers onto the property of the largely male choreographic power structure. (Satin 1996, 129)

The three women have indeed trespassed against certain conventions in traditional patriarchal dance systems and structures, specifically in classical ballet, which has been traditionally defined by the male choreographic gaze and power. Their choice of dance—borne out of various personal necessities and circumstances—as the means of telling their narratives has proved to be a potent means of their own empowerment and actualization as women and artists braving the odds of being independent from what is part of the mainstream of dance and the dominant culture. Through their dancing and with this writing, their stories are made into counter-narratives—voices that persist to be retold and reclaimed in other ways, creating cracks and crevices in the hegemonic wall of traditional dance and its historical discourse.

As a writer dancing or a dancer writing, I find that both my writing and dancing are allied performances in reinscribing independence as a mode of discourse and practice, choreographed within that interior space of memory and psyche, and performed in this public space of research and writing.

Defiance in dance—disrupting old ways of knowing and doing dance—has indeed many forms, and we have seen how the dance-makers here have taken off into various pathways while still keeping to the history and traditions that honed and grounded them in their art form. Traversing the spaces of three women dance artists, I see how these recollected memories of our storied past and hopeful present can draw up many possibilities of living and dancing out a dignified defiance as independent artists of their own making, and of our own meaningful re-making.

Bibliography

Aalten, Anna. 1997. "Performing the Body, Creating Culture." In *Embodied Practices: Feminist Perspectives on the Body*, edited by Kathy Davis. London: Sage Publications.

Adair, Christy. 1992. *Women and Dance: Slyphs and Sirens*. New York: New York University Press.

Alejandro, Reynaldo. 1978. *Philippine Dance*. Manila: Vera-Reyes.

Alejandro, Reynaldo and Amanda Abad Santos Gana. 2002. *Sayaw: Philippine Dances*. Manila: Anvil Publishing.

Banes, Sally. 1998. *Dancing Women: Female Bodies on Stage*. London and New York: Routledge.

Beltran, Myra C. 1999. "Reclaiming the Body as Home: A Rite of Passage to the 21st Century." In *1998 Philippine International Dance Conference: Dance in Revolution, Revolution in Dance*, edited by Basilio EstebanVillaruz and Leonila Bondoy. Manila: World Dance Alliance-Philippines.

Brown, Carol. 1994. "Re-tracing our steps: The possibilities for feminist dance histories." In *Dance History: An Introduction,* edited by Janet Adshead-Lansdale and June Layson. London and New York: Routledge.

———. 1997. "Dancing Between Hemispheres: Negotiating Routes for the Dancer-Academic." In *Knowing Feminisms: On Academic Borders, Territories and Tribes,* edited by Liz Stanley. London: Sage Publications.

———. 2000. "Migration and Memory: The Dances of Gertrud Bodenwieser." Conference paper presented at the Kumquat Dance Center, Philadelphia.

Burgin, Victor. 1986. *The End of Art Theory: Criticism and Postmodernity*. London: McMillan Education.

Camagay, Ma. Luisa. 2002. "Making Women Visible in History." In *Gender Sensitive and Feminist Methodologies: A Handbook for Health and Social Researchers*, edited by Sylvia Guerrero. Quezon City: University of the Philippines Press.

Carter, Alexander, ed. 1998. *The Routledge Dance Studies Reader*. London and New York: Routledge.

CCP Encyclopedia of Philippine Art. Vol. 5, *Philippine Dance*. Manila: Cultural Center of the Philippines, 1994.

Corpus, Rina Angela. 1996. "Constructing Women, Construing Dance: Reading Dancing in Mariang Sinderela and the Politics of Dance Production." Unpublished.

———. 1999. "Reading Mariang Sinderela: Towards a Feminist Discourse of Dance. *Review of Women's Studies* (University of the Philippines Center for Women's Studies) 9, vol. IX, no. 1 and 2.

———. 2000. "Two Dance-Makers in *One-Ton Pinay*: Myra Beltran and Denisa Reyes's Narratives of Dissent and Discontent." Paper for Art Studies 240. Unpublished.

———. 2003. "Defiant Daughters Dancing: Feminist Dance Histories of Three Independent Women Dance-Makers." MA thesis (Art History), University of the Philippines.

———. 2004a. "Space, Body, Woman: Dance-Making and Space-Claiming at a Studio Theater in 38 West Avenue." *Bulawan Journal of Philippine Arts and Culture,* no. 10. Manila: National Commission for Culture and the Arts.

———. 2004b. "Transgressing Cultures: Reading the Neo-ethnic in Igorot." *Bulawan Journal of Philippine Arts and Culture,* no. 14. Manila: National Commission for Culture and the Arts.

———. 2004c. "Dancing and Other Necessities: Women Seizing Spaces for an Empowering Dance Aesthetic." *Philippine Humanities Review* 7. Quezon City: College of Arts and Letters, University of the Philippines.

———. 2005. "Dancing out of the Box: Fresh Moves in Philippine Contemporary Dance." *Bulawan Journal of Philippine Arts and Culture,* no. 18. Manila: National Commission for Culture and the Arts.

Datuin, May. 1999. "Beyond the Coffee-Table: Toward a Feminist Understanding of Dance." In *1998 Philippine International Dance Conference: Dance in Revolution, Revolution in Dance,* edited by Basilio Esteban Villaruz and Leonila Bondoy. Manila: World Dance Alliance.

———. 2002. *Home Body Memory: Filipina Artists in the Visual Arts, 19th Century to the Present.* Quezon City: University of the Philippines Press.

Davis, Kathy. 1997. "Embody-ing Theory: Beyond Modernist and Postmodernist Readings of the Body." In *Embodied Practices: Feminist Perspectives on the Body*, edited by Kathy Davis. London: Sage Publications.

Desmond, Jane, ed. 1997. *Meaning in Motion: New Cultural Studies of Dance.* Durham and London: Duke University Press.

Edwards, Felicity. 1995. "Spirituality, Consciousness and Gender Identification: A Neo-Feminist Perspective." In *Religion and Gender*, edited by Ursula King. Oxford: Blackwell Publishers.

Ferne, Eric, ed. 1995. *Art History and Its Methods: A Critical Anthology*. London: Phaidon Press Ltd.

Flores, Patrick. 1997. "Philippine Painting (1521-1821) and the Politics of Colonial Visualities: Relocating the Colonial in Southeast Asian History." *SPAFA Journal* 6, no. 2.

Foster, Susan Leigh. 1986. *Reading Dancing*. Los Angeles: University of California Press.

Funk and Wagnalls New Encyclopedia. 1993 ed. S. V. "Ballet."

Hernandez, Eloisa May. 2004. *Homebound: Women Visual Artists in Nineteenth Century Philippines*. Quezon City: The University of the Philippines Press.

Goquingco, Leonor Orosa. 1980. *The Dances of the Emerald Isles*. Quezon City: Benlor Publishers.

Grosz, Elizabeth. 1994. *Volatile Bodies: Toward a Corporeal Feminism*. Indianapolis: Indiana University Press.

———. 1995. *Space, Time and Perversion: Essays on the Politics of Bodies*. New York: Routledge.

Guerrero, Sylvia, ed. 2002. *Gender Sensitive and Feminist Methodologies: A Handbook for Health and Social Researchers*. Quezon City: UP Center for Women's Studies and the University of the Philippines Press.

Guillermo, Alice, Rosa Maria Icagasi, and Elena Mirano. 1988. *Art, Man and Society*. Quezon City: UP Diliman.

Hanna, Judith Lynne. 1988a. *Dance and Stress: Resistance, Reduction and Euphoria.* New York: AMS Press, Inc.

———. 1988b. *Dance, Sex, and Gender.* Chicago: University of Chicago Press.

Joaquin, Nick. 1994. *La Orosa: The Dance Drama that is Leonor Goquinco*. Manila: Anvil Publishing and National Commission for Culture and Arts.

Jonas, Gerald. 1992. *Dancing: The Pleasure, Power, and Art of Movement.* New York: Harry N. Adams, Inc.

Layson, June. 1998. "Dance History Source Materials." In *The Routledge Dance Studies Reader*, edited by Alexander Carter. London and New York: Routledge.

Layson, June, and Janet Adshead-Lansdale, eds. 1994. *Dance History: An Introduction*. London and New York: Routledge.

Locsin, Agnes. 1999. "Transforming of Aboriginal Movement into Contemporary Choreography." In *1998 Philippine International Dance Conference: Dance in Revolution, Revolution in Dance,* edited by Basilio Esteban Villaruz and Leonila Bondoy. Manila: World Dance Alliance-Philippines.

Mojares, Resil. 1997. "Remembering the Body: Notes on Philippine Dance History." *ANI* 24. (December 1997). Manila: Cultural Center of the Philippines.

Morris, Gay. 1996. *Moving Words: Rewriting Dance*. London: Routledge.

Murray, Jan. 1979. *Dance Now: A closer look at the art of movement.* England: Penguin Books.

Ness, Sally Ann. 1992. *Body, Movement, and Culture: Kinesthetic and Visual Symbolism in a Philippine Community*. Philadelphia: University of Pennsylvania Press.

———. 1997. "Originality in the Postcolony: Choreographing the Neoethnic Body of Philippine Ballet." In *Cultural Anthropology*. American Anthropological Association.

Pollock, Griselda. 1988. "Feminist Interventions in the Histories of Art." In *Art History and its Methods: A Critical Anthology,* edited by Eric Ferne. London: Phaidon Press Ltd., 1995.

———. 1996a. *Generations and Geographies in the Visual Arts: Feminist Readings,* edited by Griselda Pollock. London and New York: Routledge.

———. 1996b. "The View from Elsewhere: Extracts from a Semi-Public Correspondence about the Visibility of Desire." In *12 Views of Manet's Bar,* edited by Bradford Collins. New Jersey: Princeton University Press.

Rivera Mirano, Elena et al. 1989. *Subli: Isang Sayaw sa Apat na Tinig*. Manila: CCP.

Satin, Leslie. 1996. "Being Danced Again: Meredith Monk, Reclaiming the Girlchild." In *Moving Words: Rewriting Dance,* edited by Gay Morris. London and New York: Routledge.

Sayers, Leslie Anne. 1997. "Madame Smudge, Some Fossils, and Other Missing Links: Unearthing the Ballet Class." In *Dance in the City,* edited by Helen Thomas. London: MacMillan Press.

Shapiro, Sherry. 1995. *Dance, Modernity and Culture: Explorations in the Sociology of Dance.* New York: Routledge.

———. 1997. *Dance in the City.* London: MacMillan Press.

———. 1998. *Dance, Power, and Difference: Critical and Feminist Perspectives on Dance Education,* edited by S. Shapiro. Illinois: Human Kinetics Publishers, Inc.

Thomas, Helen. 1995. *Dance, Modernity and Culture.* London: Routledge.

Villaruz, Basilio Esteban. 1999. "Ballet Bias: Social Clash and Compromise." In *1998 Philippine International Dance Conference: Dance in Revolution, Revolution in Dance,* edited by Basilio Esteban Villaruz and Leonila Bondoy. Manila: World Dance Alliance-Philippines.

———. 1999. "Who Writes Dance History." In *1998 Philippine International Dance Conference: Dance in Revolution, Revolution in Dance,* edited by Basilio Esteban Villaruz and Leonila Bondoy. Manila: World Dance Alliance-Philippines.

Ward, Andrew. 1997. "Dancing around Meaning (and the Meaning around Dance)." In *Dance in the City,* edited by Helen Thomas. London: MacMillan Press.

Wright, Astri. 1999a. "Self-Taught All the Way: Three Contemporary Women Artists in Indonesia." In *Proceedings of the Conference Women Imaging Women: Home, Body, Memory.* March 1999, edited by Flaudette May Datuin and Patrick Flores. Manila: Art Studies Foundation and Japan Foundation.

———. 1999b. "Self Taught Against the Grain: Three Artists and a Writer." In *Women Imaging Women: Home, Body, Memory,* edited by Flaudette May Datuin and Patrick Flores. Quezon City: Art Studies Foundation.

Articles

Anderson, Jack. 1991. "Delicacy as a Form of Spiritual Armor." *The New York Times* (September 7).

———. 1994. "Choreographer's Solos Change with Performer." *The New York Times* (September 13).

———. 1998. "Gentle Memories of a Savage War." *The New York Times* (October 13).

Chin, Gwin Joh. 1990. "Spirit Lake." *The Village Voice* (June 12).

Dakudao, Michael Ebro. 2000. "The Irrepresible Agnes Locsin." *Sunstar Davao* (April 2).

Dunning, Jennifer. 1989. "Serenity and Bellicosity in Jackson-Tanabe Bill." *The New York Times* (April 9).

———. 2001. "Evoking Other Tiny Worlds with Soft Understatement." *The New York Times* (January 8).

Gener, Randy. 1993. "A Minimalist from Malate." *Filipinas Magazine* (April issue).

Jackson, Kristin, and Keiko Fujie. 1998. "In Their Shoes" Dance Performance, Program-Brochure (October 7).

Jowitt, Deborah.1991. "Over and Over." *The New York Times* (September 24).

———. 1994. "Kristin Jackson Dance at Dia Center for the Arts." *The Village Voice* (September 27).

Kwan, SanSan. 1998. "Kristin Jackson." *Dialogue: Asian American Arts Alliance* (Fall).

Shin, Paul H.B. 1997. "Asian-Americans bare troubled lives in WWII." *Daily News* (December 31).

Sloat, Susanna. Fall 1994/Winter 1995. "Island Pulo—Kristin Jackson." *Attitude Magazine.*

Villaruz, Basilio Esteban. 1993. "Inner Landscapes." *Sunday Chronicle* (October 10).

Interviews

Beltran, Myra. 2000, 2002, 2004. 38 West Avenue, Quezon City. Interviews. 14 March 2000; 27 September 2000; 8 October 2002; March, May, June 2004.

Fabros, Mercy. 2000. Interview. 1 April 2000.

Jackson, Kristin. 2003. Quezon City. Interviews. 20 January and 11 February 2003.

Ko de la Calzada, Joanne. 2000. Interview. 27 March 2000.

Lawenko, Angela. 1996. UP Diliman, Quezon City. Interview. 11 September 1996.

Locsin, Agnes. 2004. Davao City. Interviews. 5-9 January 2004.

Locsin, Carmen. 2004. Davao City. Interviews. 10-11 January 2004.

Maranan, Christine. 2000. UP Diliman, Quezon City. Interview. 16 March 2000.

Sanchez, Katherine. 2002. Quezon City. Interview. 8 October 2002.

Videos

Igorot. CCP Library. No bibliographical data available.

Sayaw Likhang Kiukok. Agnes Locsin Collection. No bibliographical data available.

Starmaiden. Myra Beltran Collection. No bibliographical data available.

Threshold. Kristin Jackson Collection. No bibliographical data available.

Correspondences and Journals

Beltran, Myra. Letters and diary entry. 22 September 2000; 25 December 2003; 2 May 2004; 22 and 24 October 2006.

Jackson, Kristin. Letters. 2 June 2003; 21 February 2004; 22 March 2004; 11 May 2004.

Lawenko, Angela. Letter. 26 May 2004.

Locsin, Agnes. Letter. April 2004.

Websites

www.danceuk.org/services/IDAN.htm

www.mbeltrandanceforum.com/

About the Author

Rina Angela Corpus is an Assistant Professor of the Department of Art Studies at the University of the Philippines-Diliman where she finished her BA in Art Studies (1997) and MA in Art History (2004). She formerly trained and danced with the Quezon City Ballet and served as cultural editor of the *Philippine Collegian* in 1997. She is currently a contributing writer for *Women's Feature Service*. Her articles on women, art, and dance have appeared in the *Philippine Humanities Review, Bulawan*, and *Diliman Review*.